Mitt Romney
vs.
Newt Gingrich
On The Issues

**Jesse Gordon,
OnTheIssues.org**

Table of Contents

Romney vs. Gingrich on International Issues.....113

Book reviews 149

Romney vs. Gingrich on VoteMatch: 162

Mitt Romney vs. Newt Gingrich On the Issues

Former Governor Mitt Romney and Former Speaker of the House Newt Gingrich agree on some issues and disagree on many others. This book outlines their stances on the issues, in a side-by-side manner for each issue, on many of controversial topics that they will face as President.

The conventional wisdom holds that Gingrich is the "conservative alternative" to Romney. This book explores whether Gingrich is, in fact, the conservative alternative—the two candidates don't differ so much on their issue stances as they do on their focus and attitude.

We gather the two candidates' issue stances from their political autobiographies and biographies; from debates in both the 2012 election season and past elections; from public speeches; from campaign websites; and from political analysis websites. All of the excerpts appear, with many additional issue stances, on our website, www.OnTheIssues.org.

Romney ran Bain Capital and then ran the Olympics. Gingrich is best known for leading the Republican takeover of the House of Representatives in 1994 via the "Contract With America." Some pundits claim that the solution to the Great Recession requires a business perspective—in other words, that Romney's time has come. Other pundits claim that the solution is a strong conservative movement—in other words, that Gingrich's time has come again. This book lets you decide for yourself.

—Jesse Gordon, Editor-in-Chief, jesse@OnTheIssues.org
February 2012

Dedication

To Naomi

Acknowledgments

This book would not have been possible without the tireless efforts of the entire OnTheIssues team: Derek Camara, Janice Gordon, Michele Gordon, Peter Hoerr, Ram Lau, Adam Leighton, Jamie Leighton, Naomi Lichtenberg, Ogden Porter, Will Rico, Dan Teittinen, Irma Teittinen, and especially Kathleen Camara.

Romney vs. Gingrich on Domestic Issues

Domestic issues focus on joint state-federal jurisdiction or enforcement. Gingrich and Romney agree on some of these issues, but many of their disagreements occur in this section:

- *Gun Control:* Speaker Gingrich follows the hard-line conservative approach to the Second Amendment; Gov. Romney acknowledges the individual right to gun ownership, but with numerous exceptions and local restrictions.

- *Crime:* including mandatory sentencing and the death penalty. Both Gingrich and Romney support both on law-and-order grounds, but don't emphasize these issues in their campaigns.

- *Drugs:* including marijuana legalization and the War on Drugs. Romney's law enforcement-focused policy compares with Gingrich's moral basis for opposition.

- *Environment:* including pollution nuclear waste issues (also see wider energy issues in the International Issues section). Both Romney and Gingrich express support for environmental goals, but neither focuses on the issue.

- *Technology and Infrastructure:* including high-tech Internet and space issues, as well as low-tech roads and bridges investment issues. Gingrich envisions a permanent moon base; Romney is unenthused about the moon. Gingrich similarly envisions large-scale transportation projects; wants to invest directly in infrastructure; Romney echoes those goals with wariness about financing them.

- *Health Care:* including federal healthcare and ObamaCare issues; plus Medicare/Medicaid and state issues. The two candidates agree on repealing ObamaCare but differ greatly in their interpretation of RomneyCare.

Mitt Romney on Domestic Issues

Newt Gingrich on Domestic Issues

Romney on Gun Rights

Ok to ban lethal weapons that threaten police

Q: Are you still for the Brady Bill?

A: The Brady Bill has changed over time, and, of course, technology has changed over time. I would have supported the original assault weapon ban. I signed an assault weapon ban in Massachusetts governor because it provided for a relaxation of licensing requirements for gun owners in Massachusetts, which was a big plus. And so both the pro-gun and the anti-gun lobby came together with a bill, and I signed that. And if there is determined to be, from time to time, a weapon of such lethality that it poses a grave risk to our law enforcement personnel, that's something I would consider signing. There's nothing of that nature that's being proposed today in Washington. But I would look at weapons that pose extraordinary lethality.

We should check on the backgrounds of people who are trying to purchase guns. We also should keep weapons of unusual lethality from being on the street. And finally, we should go after people who use guns in the commission of crimes or illegally, but we should not interfere with the right of law-abiding citizens to own guns, for their own personal protection or hunting or any other lawful purpose. I support the work of the NRA. I'm a member of the NRA. But do we line up on every issue? No, we don't.

Source: Meet the Press: 2007 "Meet the Candidates" series,
Dec. 16, 2007

Gingrich on Gun Rights

Don't redefine Constitution
with no individual right to arms

Over the last 50 years the Supreme Court has become a permanent constitutional convention in which the whims of five appointed lawyers have rewritten the meaning of the Constitution. Under this new, all-powerful model of the Court—and by extension the trail-breaking 9th Circuit Court—the Constitution and the law can be redefined, unchecked, by federal judges.

Anyone who thinks various Supreme Court decisions are not adequately worrisome need only look at the 9th Circuit Court of Appeals to see how domination by secular Left-liberal judges will change America. It is hard to imagine that one court could be so out of step with the views of the vast majority of the American people. And it is unforgivable that this destructive pattern could have been going on for a generation without an effective challenge.

For example, consider the following 9th Court decision: *Silveira v. Lockyear*, (2002): The 9th Circuit held there is no individual right to keep and bear arms.

Source: *Winning the Future, by Newt Gingrich, pp. 57-9, Oct. 1, 2005*

NOTE: The "9th Circuit Court" refers to a federal court which is inferior to the Supreme Court. The Supreme Court later ruled on the issue of "individual rights," in the 2008 case called "*District of Columbia v. Heller*," that the 2nd Amendment does define an individual right to gun ownership, as opposed to a "collective right" for a state-run and state-armed National Guard.

Romney on Alternative Sentencing

One Strike, You're Ours: lifetime GPS tracking

Governor Romney announced that he would propose a "One Strike, You're Ours" law for those convicted of preying on children using the Internet. Massachusetts Republican District Attorneys and Sheriffs support Governor Romney's proposal for stiff mandatory jail time to be followed by lifetime tracking by Global Positioning Satellite (GPS) for first-time offenders: "As Governor of Massachusetts, Mitt Romney was a strong defender of children. He led the effort to put photos of the state's most dangerous sex offenders on the Internet and made it easier to extend civil commitments for sex offenders.

As a candidate for president, Governor Romney is once-again demonstrating strong leadership in protecting our children. His 'One Strike, You're Ours' law is an important initiative to strengthen law enforcement and protect America's sons and daughters. We are proud to stand alongside Governor Romney in his campaign for our nation's highest office.

Source: Press Release, "Law Enforcement Officials," July 21, 2007

NOTE: "Three Strikes" laws mandate that criminal offenders are sentenced to life imprisonment upon their third criminal conviction. The term refers to the baseball rule, "Three Strikes and You're Out." Romney's term "One Strike" is intended to be a stricter version of Three Strikes.

Gingrich on Alternative Sentencing

3-strike laws are constitutional; enforce courts compliance

Anyone who thinks the various decisions of the Supreme Court are not adequately worrisome need only look at the Ninth Circuit Court of Appeals to see how far the Left-liberals will go and how domination by secular Left-liberal judges will change America.

For example, consider the following Ninth Court decisions:

- *Andrade v. Attorney General of California*, (2001): The Ninth Circuit said the California three-strikes law was unconstitutional; the Supreme Court reversed it.

- *Summerlin v. Stewart*, (2003): The Ninth Circuit ruled that death sentences must be enacted by a jury, and not a judge, and that the ruling applied retroactively, voiding the death sentences of over 100 inmates. The Supreme Court reversed the retroactive ruling.

When a court is reversed this often, it clearly fails to meet the "good behavior" test of the Constitution. The good behavior test should be enforced. It would certainly focus the Ninth Circuit's attention on survival rather than radicalism.

Source: Winning the Future, by Newt Gingrich, pp. 58-60, Oct. 1, 2005

Romney on Death Penalty

Supports death penalty in heinous murders

Romney pushes for a death penalty law for murderers convicted of heinous first-degree homicides. "The ultimate penalty should be available in Massachusetts for criminals who commit the most egregious murders," Romney said.

Source: Campaign web site, www.romney2002.com, "Issues,"
Sept. 17, 2002

Favored stricter sentencing and death penalty

- Supported death penalty

- Wanted to abolish parole, limit probation, and end furloughs and release programs for violent or repeat offenders

- Favored mandatory sentencing and three strikes and you're out

- Supported restrictions on plea bargaining

- His crime prevention efforts also focused on instilling family values.

Source: Boston Globe review of 1994 campaign issues, March 21, 2002

Gingrich on Death Penalty

Voted NO on replacing death penalty with life imprisonment

Amendment to replace death penalty crimes in the 1994 Omnibus Crime Bill with life imprisonment.

Source: Bill HR 4092; vote number 107 on April 14, 1994

More prisons, more enforcement, effective death penalty

Gingrich wrote the Contract with America:

[As part of the Contract with America, within 100 days we pledge to bring to the House Floor the following bill]:

The Taking Back Our Streets Act: An anti-crime package including stronger truth in sentencing, "good faith" exclusionary rule exemptions, effective death penalty provisions, and cuts in social spending from this summer's crime bill to fund prison construction and additional law enforcement to keep people secure in their neighborhoods and kids safe in their schools.

Source: Contract with America on Sept. 27, 1994

NOTE: The death penalty is currently implemented in 34 states. It was re-legalized by a Supreme Court decision in 1977. Since then, 1,278 people have been executed. About 3,250 inmates remain on 'Death Row.' Texas is by far the national leader in executions—it has executed 477 people as of Jan. 2012, 37% of the national total. (Virginia is a very distant second with 109).

Romney on Drugs in Society

Combat the ruthless narco-terrorists in Colombia

On the 197th anniversary of Colombia's independence, we honor the many contributions that Colombian-Americans have made to our country. We also express our abiding solidarity with the Colombian people, who are fighting to secure their country's future from leftist guerrillas and narco-terrorists who have thrived on terror, violence and corruption for too many years.

A safe and prosperous Western Hemisphere requires a strong and democratic Colombia. The US must continue to provide strong support for Colombia's efforts to combat the ruthless narco-terrorists that operate there. Our partnership with Colombia contributes to our security and our quality of life—sowing stability in a critical region and helping keep deadly drugs off our streets. We can and must consolidate the gains we have made in Colombia by strengthening the economic ties between our countries. The U.S. Congress must treat this vital ally with the respect Colombia deserves and move forward now with the free trade agreement.

Source: Press Release, "Colombia Independence Day," July 20, 2007

NOTE: The U.S. "partnership with Colombia" refers to the U.S. policy called "Plan Colombia." Under Plan Colombia, the U.S. provides international aid to the government of Colombia in exchange for aerial spraying of cocaine crops and other anti-narcotic activities. Opponents describe "Plan Colombia" as a disguised means of supporting the right-wing government of Colombia, and destroying local farmers to get at the left-wing rebels known as FARC (Revolutionary Armed Forces of Colombia).

Gingrich on Drugs in Society

Drug-free society
focuses on both drug supply & demand

It is essential that we find the means to create a drug-free society for our children. As everyone knows, this has not been an easy matter for us.

The Partnership for a Drug-Free America, with its constant efforts at persuasion & education, and Nancy Reagan's "Just Say No" campaign had a real effect on drug use between 1984 and 1992. In fact, drug use declined by 2/3 in 8 years. Drug use began to rise again when the educational ad campaigns were dumped by the Clinton Administration. Now we have to launch a full-scale torrent of antidrug education, in schools, in churches, in youth organizations, in after-school programs, and everywhere else that young people hang out.

We must also raise the cost of buying and using drugs. We must find a number of economic and social penalties—not just the threat of prison which we know does not work—that will make drug use socially unacceptable. We must seal off the American border by combining [various agencies] into one focused border agency.

Source: Lessons Learned the Hard Way, by Newt Gingrich, pp.204-205,
Jul 2, 1998

Romney on Marijuana Legalization

Opposes legalization of
recreational or medical marijuana

The former Massachusetts governor opposes the legalization of recreational or medical marijuana, although he endorsed the use of synthetic pot. In his most recent book, *No Apology*, he attributes the legalization movement to "the passion and zeal of those members of the pleasure-seeking generation that never grew up."

Source: Tim Murphy in Mother Jones magazine, Apr. 20, 2011

NOTE: Medical marijuana is legal or partially legal in 18 states as of 2012: Alaska, Arizona, California, Colorado, District of Columbia, Hawaii, Maine, Maryland, Michigan, Montana, Nevada, New Jersey, New Mexico, Oregon, Rhode Island, Vermont, Virginia, and Washington. Medical marijuana is also legal in numerous foreign countries. Medical marijuana alleviates symptoms associated with glaucoma, cancer, HIV/AIDS, and numerous mental diseases.

Gingrich on Marijuana Legalization

Marijuana legalization would tear America apart

Gingrich now says that pot legalization would tear America apart: "Every place drugs are legalized the net effect is more people on welfare, more people who are dependent, more people with bad health care outcomes, fewer people who are able workers able to pay attention on the job and a drain of money into illegality, because immediately behind legalized marijuana comes cocaine and heroin.

Source: Tim Murphy in Mother Jones magazine, April 20, 2011

Admitted to smoking marijuana, coming of age in 1960s

It has been popular to conjure up in just how many ways Newt Gingrich is like Bill Clinton. Superficially they share much. Both came of age around the same time—the '60s, the Vietnam era. Each owns a vintage '60s Mustang. Each admitted to smoking marijuana and neither served in the military. Each is an indefatigable politician who has come back from crushing defeat.

Source: Newt!, by Dick Williams, p. 19, June 1, 1995

Romney on Environmental Philosophy

Clean environment will be a campaign theme

Seizing on the momentum of his successful leadership of the Olympics in Salt Lake City, Romney revealed a campaign theme that relies heavily on his management and leadership experience.

"There have been too many left behind," Romney said after his announcement, in response to reporters' questions. "Our schools aren't solid enough; our environment has not been cleaned the way it could be. Our streets are not as safe as they could be. All these things could be made better in my view with the application of new leadership and sound management principles."

The millionaire venture capitalist said voters should not have trouble connecting with his candidacy. "Everything I've done over the last three years, I think, makes it clear that I'm very much connected with the people of our country and the people of our world," he said.

Source: Stephanie Ebbert, Boston Globe, p. B6, Mar. 20, 2002

Gingrich on Environmental Philosophy

Combine healthy environment and a healthy economy

It is possible to have a healthy environment & a healthy economy. It is possible to build incentives for a cleaner future. It is possible to have biodiversity & wealthy human beings on the same planet. And it is possible to have free markets, scientific and technological advances, and an even more positive environmental outcome. There is every reason to be optimistic that if we develop smart environmental and biodiversity policies our children & grandchildren will experience an even more pleasant world.

Source: Gingrich Communications website, www.newt.org, Dec. 1, 2006

Romney on Nuclear Waste

Compensate Nevada for nuclear waste in Yucca Mountain

Q: [to Paul]: Do you support opening the national nuclear repository at Yucca Mountain?

PAUL: I've opposed this. I approach it from a state's rights position. What right does 49 states have to punish one state and say, "We're going to put our garbage in your state"?

ROMNEY: I don't always agree with Rep. Paul, but I do on that. The idea that 49 states can tell Nevada, "We want to give you our nuclear waste," doesn't make a lot of sense. I think the people of Nevada ought to have the final say as to whether they want that, and my guess is that for them to say yes, someone's going to have to offer them a pretty good deal, as opposed to having the federal government jam it down their throat. And if Nevada says, "Look, we don't want it," then let other states make bids and say, hey, look, we'll take it; here's the compensation we want for taking it. Let the free market work. And where the people say the deal's a good one will decide where we put this stuff.

Source: Primary debate in Las Vegas, Oct. 18, 2011

NOTE: Yucca Mountain is a federally-owned mountain in Nevada which the federal government has proposed as a long-term repository for nuclear waste. Yucca Mountain was selected because, in theory, it is geologically stable enough to survive intact for the thousands of years until the nuclear waste becomes harmless. The site was first proposed under Pres. Reagan in 1985-1987; Congress approved it under Pres. Bush in 2002; and then Congress canceled the program under Pres. Obama in April 2011.

Gingrich on Nuclear Waste

Put nuclear waste in deep storage for 10,000 years

Q: Do you support opening the national nuclear repository at Yucca Mountain?

GINGRICH: I think that it has to be looked at scientifically. We have to find a safe method of taking care of nuclear waste. Today, because it's been caught up in a political fight, we have small units of nuclear waste all over this country in a way that is vastly more dangerous than finding a method of keeping it in a very, very deep place that would be able to sustain 10,000 or 20,000 or 30,000 years of geological safety.

Q: Is Yucca Mountain that place?

GINGRICH: I'm not a scientist. I mean, Yucca Mountain certainly was picked by the scientific community as one of the safest places in the US.

Q: You were for opening it in Congress, right?

GINGRICH: When I was in Congress, I worked with the Nevada delegation to make sure that there was time for scientific studies. But we have to find some method of finding a very geologically stable place, and most geologists believe that, in fact, Yucca Mountain is that.

Source: GOP primary debate in Las Vegas, Oct. 18, 2011

Romney on EPA Regulations

States should be able to have their own emissions standards

Q: Gov. Schwarzenegger has proposed that California be allowed to implement much tougher environmental regulations on emission requirements than apply to the rest of the country. Do you side with the governor or with the Bush administration?

A: I side with states to be able to make their own regulations with regards to emissions within their own states. I side with states being able to make their own decisions, even if I don't always agree with the decisions they make.

Source: 2008 Republican debate at Reagan Library in Simi Valley, Jan. 30, 2008

Gingrich on EPA Regulations

Replace EPA with new Environmental Solutions Agency

I don't think the EPA bureaucrats, who are dedicated to a Washington centered, top down, bureaucratic control by litigation and regulation, are going learn a new approach, and a new model.

Now a new Environmental Solutions Agency, I believe, would do a better job of both protecting the environment and the economy. I believe that incentives, innovators, and entrepreneurs will solve environmental problems.

The new Environmental Solutions Agency should see communities, states, and industries as partners, not adversaries in solving problems when one approaches. The Environmental Solutions Agency should look for new science, new technologies, and new approaches to get more energy, more jobs, and a better environment simultaneously.

Source: Speech at Conservative Political Action Conference, Feb. 11, 2011

EPA should not regulate dust storms in Iowa

If you look at the EPA's record, it is increasingly radical, it's increasingly imperious, it doesn't cooperate, it doesn't collaborate, and it doesn't take into account economics. In Iowa they had a dust regulation under way because they control particulate matter. They were worried that the plowing of a cornfield would lead dust to go to another farmer's cornfield, and they were planning to issue a regulation. Now, this is an agency out of touch with reality, and you need a new agency that is practical, uses economic factors, and actually incentivizes change, doesn't just punish it.

Source: Meet the Press GOP New Hampshire debate, Jan. 8, 2012

Romney on Infrastructure Investment

Invest in infrastructure from growing economy by lower taxes

Q: Do you want to raise taxes to fix more bridges? Or can we cut taxes to fix more bridges?

A: There's no question—if you really want to make some money in this country, really get some money so we can repair our infrastructure and build for the future, the biggest source of that is a growing American economy. If the economy is growing slowly, when tax revenues hardly move at all, and, boy, you better raise taxes to get more money for all the things you want to do. But if the economy is growing quickly, then we generate all sorts of new revenue. And the best way to keep the economy rolling is to keep our taxes down. Our bridges—let me tell you what we did in our state. We found that we had 500 bridges, roughly, that were deemed structurally deficient. And so we changed how we focused our money. Instead of spending it to build new projects—the bridge to nowhere, new trophies for congressmen—we instead said, "Fix it first." We have to reorient how we spend our money.

Source: GOP Iowa Straw Poll debate, Aug. 5, 2007

Gingrich on Infrastructure Investment

We can't compete with China
with an inferior infrastructure

Q: What about infrastructure & job creation?

GINGRICH: Let's stick with infrastructure, because I think it's a very big, very important topic. You cannot compete with China in the long run if you have an inferior infrastructure. You've got to move to a 21st century model. That means you've got to be technologically smart and you have to make investments.

So for example here [in N.H.], the Northern Pass project ought to be buried and should be along the state's right of way. Which means you'd need these modern techniques to bring electricity from Quebec all the way down to Boston in a way that also preserves the beauty of northern New Hampshire.

[We need] the ability to have an infrastructure investment program that would actually get us back on track. If you don't have some systematic investment program, then you are not going to be able, I think, to compete with China and India.

Source: WMUR GOP New Hampshire debate, Jan. 7, 2012

Romney on Transportation Policy

A road project isn't going to stimulate the economy now

There's no question but that investment in infrastructure makes enormous sense for our country. It's good for business, it's good for the economy, and as the governor that watched almost the completion of the Big Dig, I don't know how many governors watched that $15 billion project. They do create a lot of good jobs and they help our economy. They're great things. But, unfortunately, a road project isn't going to stimulate the economy to the timeframe we have right now at the tipping point.

Source: Republican debate at Reagan Library in Simi Valley, Jan. 30, 2008

NOTE: The "Big Dig" refers to Boston's Central Artery/Tunnel Project, which converted an elevated highway, I-93, into a 3.5 mile tunnel through central Boston, and added a third tunnel under Boston Harbor to Logan Airport. The original cost of the project in 1998 was proposed at $3 billion; it grew into a $22 billion project by the latest 2012 estimate. In addition to several construction deaths, a motorist was killed when a section of ceiling collapsed in 2006, attributed to inappropriate glue to hold up the concrete ceiling. The project was also plagued by water leaks for several years, attributed to failure to meet contract specifications.

Gingrich on Transportation Policy

Establish three high-speed rail corridors; NY-MA; FL; & CA

The French & Japanese have made substantial investments in creating high-speed rail corridors. The Chinese are now following their lead. The US has 3 corridors that are very conducive to this kind of high-speed train investment. We could build a system between Boston and Washington; from Miami to Tampa, Orlando and Jacksonville; and from San Diego to San Francisco.

There are three problems with trying to build high-speed systems in the US and, not surprisingly, all three relate to government.

1. Union work rules make it impossible, at least if Amtrak has anything to do with it.

2. Pork barrel politicians waste money subsidizing absurdly uneconomic routes

3. Regulations and litigation involved in large-scale construction have become time- consuming and expensive.

I support a 21st century rail system that is privately built, run efficiently, and capable of earning its own way. The US should have a railroad system that works for us, and not for the Amtrak bureaucracy and their unions.

Source: Real Change, by Newt Gingrich, pp.211-2, Dec. 18, 2007

Romney on Outer Space Policy

Mining the moon costs too much

ROMNEY: Speaker Gingrich and I have a lot of places where we disagree.

Q: Why don't you name them?

ROMNEY: We can start with his idea to have a lunar colony that would mine minerals from the moon, I'm not in favor of spending that kind of money to do that.

GINGRICH: I'm proud of trying to find things that give young people a reason to study science and math and technology and telling them that someday in their lifetime, they could dream of going to the moon, they could dream of going to Mars. I grew up in a generation where the space program was real, where it was important, and where frankly it is tragic that NASA has been so bureaucratized. Iowa's doing brilliant things, attracting brilliant students. I want to give them places to go and things to do. And I'm happy to defend the idea that America should be in space and should be there in an aggressive, entrepreneurial way.

Source: Yahoo's "Your Voice Your Vote" debate in Iowa,
Dec. 10, 2011

Gingrich on Outer Space Policy

Get an American on the moon
before the Chinese get there

Q: [to Romney]: Speaker Gingrich said that by the end of his second term, there would be a permanent base on the moon. Good idea?

ROMNEY: That's an enormous expense. And right now I want to be spending money here.

Q: [to Gingrich]: How do you plan to create a base on the moon in eight years while keeping taxes down?

GINGRICH: You start with the question, do you really believe NASA in its current form is the most effective way of leveraging investment in space? My point is, I believe by the use of prizes, by the use of incentives, by opening up the space port so that it's available on a ready basis for commercial fight—there are many things you can do to leverage accelerating the development of space. Lindbergh flew to Paris for a $25,000 prize. If we had a handful of serious prizes, you'd see an extraordinary number of people out there trying to get to the moon first. And I'd like to have an American on the moon before the Chinese get there.

Source: CNN GOP primary debate on the eve of Florida primary,
Jan. 26, 2012

Romney on R&D Spending

National R&D spending OK; picking winners not OK

Government funding for basic science and research in universities and research laboratories has been declining for years. It needs to grow instead, particularly in engineering and the physical sciences. Research in energy, materials science, nanotechnology, and transportation are vital to the economy and to our nation's competitiveness. Government should not, however, attempt to pick winning ideas or technologies in which it would invest funds for development and commercialization.

The realities of that marketplace sort out those that have potential for growth and sustainability and those that do not. Attempting to substitute government for the roles carried out by entrepreneurs, angel investors, and venture capitalists while also bypassing the unforgiving test of the free market is a very bad idea indeed.

Source: No Apology, by Mitt Romney, pp.124-5, March 2, 2010

Gingrich on R&D Spending

Create tax incentives that encourage R&D

We should create tax incentives that encourage research and development. The 50 percent research and development tax credit should be made permanent and be applied to companies that are willing to take on government's "grand challenges" (for example, the first inhabitable moon base).

Investments in new technology and machinery should also be expensed 100 percent in the first year. The present complex code of depreciation makes no sense in a time of rapid change. It is better to encourage overinvestment in new technology and new machinery to keep American workers at the cutting edge of opportunity.

Our goal should be to ensure that American workers have newer, better, and more productive equipment than their foreign counterparts.

Source: Gingrich Communications website, www.newt.org, "Issues,"
Sep 1, 2007

Romney on Internet Policy

SOPA, as written, restricts the Internet & free speech

Q: SOPA and PIPA would crack down on Internet piracy. But opponents say it's censorship.

GINGRICH: Virtually everybody who's technologically advanced say this is going to totally mess up the Internet, and the bill in its current form is written really badly and leads to a range of censorship that is totally unacceptable.

ROMNEY: I think he got it just about right. The law as written is far too intrusive, far too expansive, far too threatening to freedom of speech and movement of information across the Internet. It would have a potentially depressing impact on one of the fastest-growing industries in America, which is the Internet and all those industries connected to it. At the same time, we care very deeply about intellectual content that's going across the Internet. And if we can find a way to very narrowly, through our current laws, go after those people who are pirating, particularly those from offshore, we'll do that—but a very broad law—I think that's a mistake.

Source: South Carolina GOP debate hosted by CNN's John King,
Jan 19, 2012

Gingrich on Internet Policy

I favor Internet freedom,
even though SOPA favors Hollywood

Q: SOPA, the Stop Online Piracy Act, would crack down on Internet piracy. But opponents say it's censorship. Our parent company, Time Warner, says we need a law like this because movies are being ripped off online. There's two competing engines of our economy at odds.

GINGRICH: Well, you're asking a conservative about the economic interests of Hollywood. And I'm weighing it.... Virtually everybody who's technologically advanced, including Google and YouTube and Facebook, say this is going to totally mess up the Internet, and the bill in its current form is written really badly and leads to a range of censorship that is totally unacceptable. Well, I favor freedom. We have a Patent Office, we have copyright law. If a company finds that it has genuinely been infringed upon, it has the right to sue, but the idea that we're going to preemptively have the government start censoring the Internet on behalf of giant corporations' economic interests strikes me as exactly the wrong thing to do.

Source: South Carolina GOP debate hosted by CNN's John King,
Jan 19, 2012

NOTE: "SOPA" and "PIPA" refer to two bills before Congress on Internet regulation. SOPA, the House's Stop Online Piracy Act, has 28 sponsors, and PIPA, the Senate's Protect IP Act, has 40 sponsors. Proponents claim the bills would better protect electronic copyright ("IP," or Intellectual Property); opponents argue that SOPA and PIPA would censor the Internet. Internet users and entrepreneurs oppose the two bills; google.com and wikipedia.com held a "blackout" on Jan. 18, 2012 in protest.

Romney on Health Mandate

Personal responsibility
instead of employer mandates

Q: What should we do with all the millions of people who are not insured?

A: Well, I actually got the job done. Working with people across the aisle, we said: Enough is enough. Look, the best kind of prevention you can have in health care is to have a doctor. And if someone doesn't have a doctor, doesn't have a clinic they can go to, doesn't have health insurance to be able to provide the prescription drugs they need, you can't be healthy. And you need to have health insurance for all of our citizens.

And I found a way to do that without requiring raising taxes, without a government mandate, without a government takeover. When I said government mandate, I meant employer mandate. Instead, we have personal responsibility. We allowed individuals to buy their own policies. Those that couldn't afford them, we helped them buy their policies. And you know what? It cost us no more money to help people buy insurance policies that they could afford than it was costing us before, handing out free care.

Source: Republican primary debate on Univision, Dec. 9, 2007

Gingrich on Health Mandate

If you mandate healthcare, you mandate everything in life

Q: You've been very open to the individual mandate. It has become a litmus test in this Republican primary. Should it be?

A: Yes, it should be. If you explore the mandate, it ultimately ends up with unconstitutional powers. It allows the government to define virtually everything. And if you can do it for health care, you can do it for everything in your life, and, therefore, we should not have a mandate.

But I want to answer at a different level. This campaign cannot be only about the presidency. We need to pick up at least 12 seats in the Senate and 30 or 40 more seats in the House, because if you are serious about repealing Obamacare, you have to be serious about building a big enough majority in the legislative branch that you could actually in the first 90 days pass the legislation. So I just think it's very important to understand, it's not about what one person in America does. It's about what the American people do. And that requires a senatorial majority, as well as a presidency.

Source: GOP primary debate in Manchester NH, June 13, 2011

Romney on Medicare

Reform Medicare, but don't cancel prescription program

Q: [to Perry]: If you were president, would you repeal prescription drug benefits for seniors under Medicare?

PERRY: No. But it's a $17 trillion hole that we have in our budget we've got to deal with.

Q: [to Romney] How about you?

ROMNEY: I wouldn't repeal it. I'd reform Medicare and reform Medicaid and reform Social Security to get them on a sustainable basis, not for current retirees, but for those in their 20s and 30s and early 50s.

Source: Tea Party debate in Tampa FL, Sept. 12, 2011

Get everybody insured with state-based market dynamics

The way we improve something is not by putting more government into it. In my view, instead, the right way for us to go is to bring in place the kind of market dynamics that make the rest of the economy so successful. So my plan gets everybody in America insured, takes the burden of free riders off of our auto companies and everybody else, and says let's get everybody in the system.

Instead of having the federal government give you government insurance, Medicare and federal employee insurance, let's have private insurance.

Source: Republican debate in Dearborn, Michigan, Oct. 9, 2007

Gingrich on Medicare

Block grant Medicaid; create individual incentives & bonuses

Q: What about Medicaid?

GINGRICH: Go to Newt.org for the proposed 21st Century Contract with America. The first step is to repeal Obamacare. [Then] block grant Medicaid. And block grant all remaining welfare programs. Give the states the power to deal with the poor using innovation and money savings.

I do not believe you solve problems under the Left's policy of people being helpless. We need to rethink Medicaid much the way we rethought welfare reform. Governor Bush in Florida had a program where people who took care of themselves and didn't go to the emergency room got a Christmas bonus. To the shock of academics, poor people were aware of money and strived to get that bonus by not abusing the emergency rooms.

If you had the ability to triage and send people to minute clinics, then the hospital wouldn't charge emergency room rates. We have to start distinguishing between the taxpayer who is concerned with charitable care and taxpayers who are suckers and are being exploited.

Source: Head-to-head debate between Herman Cain & Newt Gingrich,
Nov 5, 2011

Romney on ObamaCare

I stand by what I did in Massachusetts; but not ObamaCare

Q: Do you stand by what you did with the health care mandate in Massachusetts?

ROMNEY: Absolutely. I'm not running for governor. I'm running for president. And if I'm president, on day one I'll direct the secretary of Health and Human Services to grant a waiver from Obamacare to all 50 states. It's a problem that's bad law, it's not constitutional. I'll get rid of it.

Q: [to Perry]: Can a state like Massachusetts go ahead and pass health care reform, including mandates? Is that a good idea, if Massachusetts wants to do it?

PERRY: Well, that's what Gov. Romney wanted to do, so that's fine. But the fact of the matter is, that was the plan that President Obama has said himself was the model for Obamacare. I don't think it was right for Massachusetts when you look at what it's costing the people of Massachusetts today.

ROMNEY: If you think what we did in Massachusetts and what Pres. Obama did are the same, boy, take a closer look: he raised taxes $500 billion; we didn't raise taxes.

Source: Tea Party debate in Tampa FL, Sept. 12, 2011

Gingrich on ObamaCare

Repeal ObamaCare; sign tort reform instead

President Obama could be bipartisan. There are seven steps to the center for Obama.

1. Sign the repeal of ObamaCare. 58% of the American people, in the most recent poll, favor repeal of ObamaCare.

2. Sign Tort reform for doctors. He said the other night he would like to do it, let's let him do it.

3. Sign the permanent repeal of the death tax.

4. Sign a new Hyde Amendment, so no taxpayer money funds abortion in the United States.

5. Sign a new Conservative Budget Act, to control spending and move to a balanced budget.

6. Sign a law to decisively control the border now.

7. Sign a tenth amendment implementation act returning power from Washington to the states and to the people thereof. And that act should include—to prove how real it is—block-granting Medicaid so that states can control the cost and improve the quality without interference from Washington bureaucrats.

Now, I hope you'd agree with me that a President Obama that did those seven things would have come to the center.

Source: Speech at Conservative Political Action Conference,
Feb 11, 2011

Romney vs. Gingrich on Economic Issues

Economic issues focus on the recession recovery and all fiscal matters. Romney and Gingrich largely agree on these issues, whereas on social and domestic issues they often disagree:

- *Budget & Economy:* including deficit spending and all aspects of the federal budget. Gov. Romney opposes all bailouts and economic stimulus. Speaker Gingrich agrees but focuses on legislative reforms.

- *Corporations:* including corporate taxation and corporate welfare. Gingrich focuses on making businesses more efficient. Romney would reduce corporate taxes; but the campaign will focus on Romney's personal history as a corporate leader (or as a "vulture capitalist," depending on one's point of view).

- *Government Reform:* focusing on the size and role of the federal government, which Romney and Gingrich agree should be smaller and more restricted. The two candidates also agree on campaign finance: that privately-funded TV campaign ads are free speech.

- *Jobs:* including unemployment and union issues. Romney would restrict unions and limit unemployment compensation; Gingrich agrees but would address them by defunding federal agencies.

- *Social Security:* including the current Trust Fund and changes for the future. Gov. Romney would provide opt-out mechanisms; Speaker Gingrich agrees but more fervently.

- *Tax Reform:* including income taxes, tax rates, and bracket redistribution. Romney would radically reduce taxes, citing supply-side economics for corporate tax reductions, but focusing on the middle class for income tax reductions. Gingrich agrees on supply-side economics but his single-rate tax system would more favor upper-income earners.

Mitt Romney
on Economic Issues

Newt Gingrich
on Economic Issues

Romney on Corporation Policy

Corporations are people

Campaigning in Iowa, Mitt Romney told a heckler, "Corporations are people, my friend"—words immediately seized upon by Democrats in what they termed as a possible defining statement by the presidential candidate.

Romney, speaking to a crowd at the Iowa State Fair, was being pressed about raising taxes to help cover entitlement spending. When one mentioned raising corporate tax rates, Romney responded by saying corporations were no different than people. The line earned him a sustained round of applause from the crowd.

But the Democratic National Committee fired off emails almost immediately after the remarks, as part of a continuing effort to frame the GOP frontrunner as an out-of-touch elitist, writing: "This is what Mitt Romney is going to run on?

A small band of hecklers, positioned near the stage, continually quarreled with Romney about whether wealthy Americans should pay higher taxes. "There was a time in this country when we didn't attack people based on their success," Romney said.

Source: James Oliphant in the Los Angeles Times, Aug. 11, 2011

Gingrich on Corporation Policy

Businesses focus on customers; apply Lean Six Sigma to government

CAIN: You spent a lot of distinguished years in Congress and then you left Congress and started other ventures and you were thinking outside the Washington bubble. What are three things you realized outside that bubble?

GINGRICH: As a business, you don't get to stay in business unless you wake up every day thinking about how to keep customers. If you don't earn your pay in business, a business won't pay you. We need to apply Lean Six Sigma principles to government. In every aspect of the private sector someone is doing something brilliant that could be applied to government to reduce costs, but the Left and the media block this. If you found Best Practices across the country, you would be amazed at how quickly you could balance the budget and resolve the deficit. When I left office as Speaker, there was a swing of $5 *trillion* and we had a balanced budget. CEOs set big goals with tight deadlines, delegate smartly, and don't let any so-called experts in the room.

Source: Head-to-head debate between Herman Cain & Newt Gingrich,
Nov 5, 2011

NOTE: "Six Sigma" refers to a business management strategy developed by Edwards Deming in the 1980s, based on a cycle of "Plan-Do-Check-Act." The complementary "lean manufacturing" methods focus on process and waste (making work faster), where Six Sigma focuses on design (making work better). In recent years, the combined strategy has become known as "Lean Six Sigma."

Romney on Wall Street Reform

I was CEO at mainstream businesses, not Wall St.

CAIN: Gov. Romney has a very distinguished career. There's one difference between the two of us in terms of our experience. With all due respect, his business executive experience has been more Wall Street-oriented; mine has been more Main Street. I have managed small companies. I've actually had to clean the parking lot. I've worked with groups of businesses.

ROMNEY: The fact that we're both doing as well as we are is we both have a private-sector background. But I just want to set the record straight. I've been chief executive officer four times, once for a start-up and three times for turnarounds. One was a financial services company. That was the start-up. A consulting company, that's a mainstream business. The Olympics, that's certainly mainstream. And, of course, the state of Massachusetts. In all those settings, I've learned how to create jobs.

Source: Primary debate in Las Vegas, Oct. 18, 2011

Gingrich on Wall Street Reform

Dodd-Frank kills small business & small banks

Q: [to Gingrich]; Gov. Romney has said that the government should let the foreclosure process play out so that the housing market can recover and the free markets can work. Is he right?

GINGRICH: He's certainly right that you want to get to the real value of the houses as fast as you can. But I think there are two specific steps you have got to understand in terms of housing. If the Congress would repeal Dodd-Frank, you would see the housing market start to improve overnight. Dodd-Frank kills small banks, it kills small business. The federal regulators are anti-housing loan, and it has maximized the pain level. You could also change some of the rules so it would be easier to do a short sale where the house is worth less than mortgage than it is to do a foreclosure. Today, the banks are actually profiting more by foreclosing than encouraging short sales. But in the long run, you want the housing market to come back? The economy has to come back.

Source: CNBC GOP Primary debate in Rochester MI, Nov. 9, 2011

NOTE: "Dodd-Frank" refers to Sen. Chris Dodd (D, CT) and Rep. Barney Frank (D, MA), the co-authors of the Dodd–Frank Wall Street Reform and Consumer Protection Act of 2010. The legislation was intended to reform the rules of the financial and insurance industry to avoid another "meltdown" like the one in mid-2008 which initiated the Great Recession.

Romney on Automaker Bailout

TARP should not be used for auto company bailouts

I know we didn't all agree on TARP. I believe that it was necessary to prevent a cascade of bank collapses. For free markets to work, there has to be a currency and a functioning financial system. But we can agree on this: TARP should not have been used to bail out GM, Chrysler and the UAW. And this is personal for me, I want the US auto industry to succeed. But that can only happen if its excessive costs and burdens are restructured. The right answer for Detroit is this: Fix it first.

All of these measures are meant to confront the current economic peril. Properly guided, Washington could in fact speed the recovery. So far, some of the actions it has taken will help, and some will hurt. But we can be certain that the American economy will recover. The invisible hand of the market is more powerful than the lumbering machinery of government. The private sector—entrepreneurs and businesses large and small—will create the millions of jobs our country needs.

Source: Speech to Conservative Political Action Conference,
Feb. 27, 2009

NOTES: "TARP" refers to the Troubled Asset Relief Program, Pres. Bush's 2008 program to purchase assets from financial institutions to alleviate the subprime mortgage crisis. Pres. Bush approved using $17 billion in TARP funds for GM and Chrysler beginning in 2008.

Gingrich on Automaker Bailout

Bailout combines bad policy
with worst of Detroit's decay

"In an amazing display of historic ignorance, economic destructiveness, and ideologically driven dishonesty, Washington politicians are in the process of combining the worst of the 1970s bad economic policies with the worst of Detroit's economic and (America's) educational decay. We are in grave danger of turning all of America into the kind of declining economy and bureaucratic mess which Detroit became over the last forty years."—Newt Gingrich

Source: Saving Freedom, by Jim DeMint, p.124, July 4, 2009

NOTE: The federal government "bailed out" the Big Three automakers early in the 2008 Great Recession. The bailout consisted of direct loans to General Motors and Chrysler, and a line of credit for Ford Motors. President Bush's $17 billion loan to GM and Chrysler was contingent upon the two automakers following federal government restructuring of their companies. The purpose of the bailout was to avoid bankruptcy and a large surge in unemployment of auto workers.

Romney on Financial Bailout

Bailout program wasted money; let companies go bankrupt

Q: GM and Chrysler have rebounded. Would you say the bailout program was a success?

A: The bailout program was not a success because it wasted $17 billion. When the auto company CEOs went to Washington asking for money, I said the right process is not big check from Washington, but instead letting these enterprises go through bankruptcy, getting rid of the unnecessary costs, and re-emerge on their feet again. Instead, the Bush administration and the Obama administration wrote checks to the auto industry.

Q: You wrote in Nov. 2008, "If GM, Ford and Chrysler get the bailout, you can kiss the American automotive industry goodbye." Were you wrong?

A: No, I wasn't wrong, because if you read the rest of the op-ed piece, it says they need to shed unnecessary costs. If they just get federal checks, they're going to be locked in with high UAW legacy costs. They'll never be able to get on their feet. They have to go through bankruptcy. And it turned out that that's finally what they did.

Source: GOP primary debate in Manchester NH, June 13, 2011

Gingrich on Financial Bailout

Insure banks rather than pass out checks

The Path to Socialist Banking:

1. In Sep. 2008, the major brokerage houses teeter on the brink of bankruptcy.

2. President Bush and his Treasury secretary propose a huge bailout to inject $700 billion of capital into falling financial institutions to stabilize them and stop a run on their assets. The plan is called Troubled Assets Relief Program (TARP).

3. Republicans in the House try to stop the bill (they had the majority then) and substitute an approach masterminded by former House speaker Newt Gingrich to insure banks rather than pass out checks to them. The House defeats the Bush bailout proposal.

4. John McCain "suspends" his campaign; the Republicans in the House cave in at the behest of their nominee and agree to TARP.

5. Democrats ask, what will the taxpayer get out of the TARP bailouts? Had the Republicans listened to Gingrich, the question would have had no force, since no money would have changed hands. But in the context of the Bush TARP bill, the question demands an answer.

Source: Take Back America, by Dick Morris, pp.103-5, April 13, 2010

Romney on Economic Stimulus

Key to economic stimulus:
get companies to buy more stuff

Q: The president's economic stimulus plan would send out 116 million checks to American homes. The plan is somewhat contrary to yours, providing lots of short-term stimulus to individuals. Your plan focuses as much on the long term as the short term. Are you disappointed that your recipe for the economy was not embraced by the president? And will you now embrace his plan?

A: Well, there's a great deal that is effective in his plan. First, he's getting money back to consumers. That makes sense to me I just think we need to go further. We go to corporate support and helping corporations have the incentive to buy more capital equipment. That he also does. I do it more aggressively by writing off a larger amount of capital expenditures—getting companies to buy more stuff so that other companies will hire people. If you want to turn an economy around, the key thing is to grow jobs. It's not just to get checks in the hands of consumers; it's consumers & companies buying things that create jobs.

Source: GOP debate in Boca Raton Florida, Jan. 24, 2008

Gingrich on Economic Stimulus

No sequel to failed stimulus & job-killing policies

Last night President Obama called for a sequel to his failed stimulus, proving he continues to support the same destructive, job-killing policies that created the Obama Depression. If the jobs weren't shovel-ready after his $800 billion stimulus, which the president himself admitted, why will this be different?

After repeatedly calling on Congress to pass his American Jobs Act immediately—we discover there is no bill and no plan to pay for it. President Obama continues to ignore facts and instead doubles down on failed economic policies. We need real leadership now that uses proven policies from the Reagan presidency and my Speakership to empower Americans to create jobs.

Source: Response to Obama's Jobs Speech, Sept. 9, 2011

NOTES: The "American Jobs Act" refers to a series of legislative proposals made by President Obama beginning in Sept. 2011. Initially, the legislation was proposed as one large bill (S. 1549 and H.R. 12), but the bill stalled in Congress. Hence Obama broke up the bill into numerous smaller pieces. The key components are:

- $245 billion for Payroll tax cut extension (maintaining a reduction in the Social Security FICA deduction).

- $57 billion for extending unemployment benefits

- $65 billion for direct hiring of municipal employees, focusing on teachers, police, and firefighters

- $65 billion for infrastructure construction.

The term "shovel ready" refers to the previous round of stimulus bills, which focused on projects which could start immediately.

Romney on Mortgage Crisis

Fannie Mae and Freddie Mac were source of housing bubble

Q: Would you phase out Fannie Mae and Freddie Mac? Does the private mortgage industry need additional regulation?

ROMNEY: Well, I think you know that Fannie Mae and Freddie Mac were a big part of why we have the housing crisis in the nation that we have. Speaker Gingrich was hired by Freddie Mac to promote them, to influence other people throughout Washington, encouraging them not to dismantle these two entities. I think that was an enormous mistake. I think, instead, we should have had a whistle-blower and not horn-tooter. He should have stood up and said, look, these things are a disaster; this is a crisis. He should have been anxiously telling the American people that these entities were causing a housing bubble that would cause a collapse that we've seen around the country. And are they a problem today? Absolutely. They're offering mortgages, again to people who can't possibly repay them. We're creating another housing bubble, which will hurt the American people.

Source: CNN GOP primary debate on the eve of Florida primary,
Jan 26, 2012

Gingrich on Mortgage Crisis

Don't bail out Freddie Mac & Fannie Mae; break them up

Rep. PAUL: [to Gingrich]: He received a lot of money from Freddie Mac. While he was earning a lot of money from Freddie Mac, I was fighting over a decade to try to explain to people where the housing bubble was coming from. So Freddie Mac is bailed out by the tax payers. So in a way, Newt, I think you probably got some of our tax payer's money.

GINGRICH: First, the housing bubble came from the Federal Reserve inflating the money supply. Second, I was never a spokesman for any agency, I never did any lobbying for any agency. I offered strategic advice. I was in the private sector. You're allowed to charge money for it. It's called free enterprise. I'm not for bailing them out, in fact, I'm for breaking them up.

Q: Rep. Bachmann, you called Speaker Gingrich a "poster boy of crony capitalism."

BACHMANN: When you're taking over $100 million to influence the outcome of legislation in Washington, that's the epitome of a consummate insider.

Source: Yahoo's "Your Voice Your Vote" debate in Iowa, Dec. 10, 2011

NOTE: "Fannie & Freddie" refer to the Federal National Mortgage Association (FNMA, Fannie Mae) and Federal Home Loan Mortgage Corporation (FHLMC, Freddie Mac). Fannie and Freddie were "GSEs"—government-sponsored enterprises—half-private, half-federal, until 2008, when they were placed under full federal control. Their role is to assist banks with creating individual mortgages.

Romney on National Debt

The "Party of No" is ok
when it comes to spending

The president accuses us of being the party of no. It's as if he thinks that by saying no, it's by definition a bad thing. In fact, it's right and praiseworthy to say no to bad things. It's right to say no to Cap-and-trade, no to Card Check, no to government healthcare, no to higher taxes.

Our party can never be a rubber stamp for rubber-stamp spending. But before we move away from this "No" epithet that the Democrats are fond of trying to apply to us, let's ask the Obama folks why they say no: no to a balanced budget, no to reforming entitlements, no to malpractice reform, no to missile defense in eastern Europe, no to tax cuts. You see, we conservatives don't have a corner on saying no. We're just the ones who say it when it's the right thing to say.

Source: Speech to Conservative Political Action Conference,
Feb. 20, 2010

Gingrich on National Debt

Democrats say they oppose earmarks, but proposed 8,000

I listened carefully to the President's speech the other night. Obama suggests to us that he is opposed to earmarks, when the very next day the Democrats are going to bring up a bill with 8,000 earmarks in it and then to suggest that one doesn't count because they started all the pork before he got here. I was looking for change we can believe in.

And so I was startled that he was saying to us that he opposed to earmarks; [I suppose maybe] later he'll really oppose them.

Source: Speech to Conservative Political Action Conference,
Feb 27, 2009

NOTE: "Earmarks" refers to itemized spending in legislation, i.e., funding targeted toward a particular project in a particular place. The controversy comes about because often the particular place includes the home district of the legislator writing or sponsoring the bill (which is known derisively as "Pork-Barrel Spending"). Earmarks are currently legal and are generally considered ethical; earmark reform focuses on publicizing their existence and perhaps on a future Line Item Veto to remove some.

Romney on Balanced Budget

Cap how much government can spend as a percentage of GDP

If you go back a few years to JFK's time, the government at all levels—federal, state and local—was consuming about 27% of the US economy. Today it consumes about 37% of the US economy. It's on track to get to 40%. We cease at some point to be a free economy. And the idea of saying, we just want a little more, just give us some more tax revenue, we need that, that is the answer for America.

The answer is to cut federal spending. The answer is to cap how much the federal government can spend as a percentage of our economy and have a balanced budget amendment.

And the second part of the answer is to get our economy to grow, because the idea of just cutting and cutting and taxing more—I understand mathematically those things work, but nothing works as well as getting the economy going. Get Americans back to work. Get them paying taxes. Get corporations growing in America. And I'll tell you, these kinds of problems will disappear.

Source: GOP debate at Dartmouth College, NH, Oct. 11, 2011

Gingrich on Balanced Budget

Demand a Balanced Budget Amendment

Gingrich signed the Contract From America

The Contract from America, clause 3:

Demand a Balanced Budget:

Begin the Constitutional amendment process to require a balanced budget with a two-thirds majority needed for any tax hike.

The Contract from America, clause 6:

End Runaway Government Spending:

Impose a statutory cap limiting the annual growth in total federal spending to the sum of the inflation rate plus the percentage of population growth.

Source: The Contract From America, July 8, 2010

Romney on Campaign Finance Reform

McCain-Feingold hurt our party and hurt the First Amendment

Q: Back in 2002, when McCain was campaigning for you when you were running for governor of Massachusetts, you said McCain "has always stood for reform and change, and he's always fought the good battle, no matter what the odds." Now you're saying in N.H. that McCain is not an agent of change. Why have you changed your opinion?

A: Oh, I still think he's a battler for change. He's just been there 27 years and hasn't been able to get the job done. He has brought some bills in place like McCain-Feingold, which hurt our party & I think hurt the First Amendment. He fought for immigration law, which I think was a terrible course, which said that all the illegal aliens that had come here illegally would be able to stay in this country forever. That was a mistake. Washington is broken. America is saying it loud and clear. You had in Iowa a number of experienced senators going up against folks that were new faces, governors, and the experienced senators lost.

Source: Fox News interview: "Choosing the President" series, Jan. 6, 2008

NOTE: "McCain-Feingold" refers to the Bipartisan Campaign Reform Act of 2002, also known as BCRA, named after its sponsors, Sen. John McCain (R, AZ) and Sen. Russ Feingold (D, WI). McCain-Feingold doubled the campaign donation limit from $1,000 per person to $2,000 per person ($2,500 in 2012), known as "hard money." The law banned "soft money" contributions to political parties, but later Supreme Court cases, particularly "Citizens United," allowed unlimited soft money for purposes of advertising for or against a candidate as long as there was no "coordination" with the campaign.

Gingrich on Campaign Finance Reform

Increase federal limits on individual campaign contributions

Gingrich indicated the principles he would support regarding campaign finance reform:

- Support legislation that would increase the federal limits on individual contributions.

- Strengthen and enforce legislation that encourages full and timely disclosure of campaign finance information.

- Prohibit non-U.S. citizens from making contributions to federal campaigns.

Source: Congressional National Political Awareness Test,
Nov 1, 1998

Romney on Growth of Government

Make government simpler, smaller, and smarter

If tonight were the first message to Congress in a Romney administration, I'd have the courage to tell the American people how it is and tell Congress what we really need to do. I wouldn't spend my time blaming others for how we got in this mess; I'd explain how we're going to get out of it. I'd use the State of the Union to lay out an agenda that will get our country back on track and get our fiscal house in order.

My agenda would make government simpler, smaller, and smarter. As President, I will repeal unnecessary regulations and restore our good credit rating. I will reduce tax rates and simplify the tax code, especially for middle-income Americans. I will streamline regulation, ensure the prompt review of projects, and order agencies to focus on economic growth.

I would pledge to do all that a President can to get America working again. When it comes to the economy, my highest priority would be worrying about your job, not saving my own.

Source: Prebuttal to Obama's State of the Union speech, Jan. 24, 2012

Gingrich on Growth of Government

Bigger government lead to more food stamps, not more jobs

We have a crisis of work in this country and Pres. Obama proposed nothing in the way of policy changes that will get us to robust job creation and dramatic economic growth. Instead, the president described his conviction that his big government is built to last and should be paid for with higher taxes.

But bigger government and higher taxes will not lead to jobs and growth. Bigger government and higher taxes will instead lead to more people on food stamps, a situation which the President and his party defend as a fair outcome.

Economic growth and prosperity is not really at the top of Obama's agenda. He will always prefer a food stamp economy to a paycheck economy and call it fair.

For the president and a large part of the political class, it's about their power, their right to rule. That's why so much of that nearly trillion-dollar stimulus didn't create jobs but just went into the pockets of special interests who support Obama and the Democratic Party.

Source: Response to Obama's State of the Union speech, Jan. 24, 2012

Romney on Union Policy

"Card check" is a massive imposition on worker freedom

The most naked pro-union power play in decades is the AFL-CIO demand to change the process by which a union enters a company's workplace.

The proposed statute, known as "card check" legislation, would represent a massive imposition on the freedom of workers to choose whether or not to become part of a union. Currently, the decision about unionization is made by a secret-ballot vote by the company's employees, but because unions haven't been winning a lot of elections, they want to change the rules.

Under the AFL-CIO plan, the union would collect pro-unionization signature cards from a majority of employees, cards that could be collected over an extended period of time and without the knowledge of the employer that an organizing effort is under way; thus, employees could be targeted and pressured, one by one.

This is a remarkable departure from the one of the prerequisites of any democracy—that of a secret ballot. It's easy to imagine how this system could lead to employee harassment and coercion.

Source: No Apology, by Mitt Romney, pp.112-3, March 2, 2010

NOTE: "Card Check" refers to a unionization process where potential union members sign (or check off) a card indicating they would join the union. When a majority of workers have checked their cards, the union forms. Mitt Romney and most Republicans argue that Card Check inappropriately replaces a secret ballot process, and is inherently coercive.

Gingrich on Union Policy

Defund National Labor Relations Board; favor right-to-work

Q: New Hampshire could soon become the 23rd state to pass right to work legislation. Unions don't like it because it makes membership voluntary. Would you support a federal right-to-work law?

A: One of the things the Congress should do immediately is defund the National Labor Relations Board which has gone into South Carolina to punish Boeing, which wants to put 8,000 American jobs in S.C. by fundamentally eliminating right-to-work at the National Labor Relations Board. That's a real, immediate threat from the Obama administration to eliminate right to work. And I think that it is fundamentally the wrong direction. I hope that New Hampshire does adopt right-to-work. I frankly keep it at the state level because as each new state becomes right to work, they send a signal to the remaining states, don't be stupid. If you believe in the 10th Amendment, we ought to let the states learn from each other. And the right-to-work states are creating a lot more jobs today that they heavily unionized states.

Source: GOP primary debate in Manchester NH, June 13, 2011

Romney on Unemployment

Replace jobless benefits with unemployment savings accounts

Q: You've suggested replacing government jobless benefits with individual unemployment savings accounts. Jobless benefits for millions of Americans are about to expire; would you extend them?

A: Unemployment benefits, I think they've gone on a long, long time. But I would rather see a reform of our unemployment system, to allow people to have a personal account which they're able to draw from as opposed to having endless unemployment benefits. Let's reform the system, make the system work better by giving people responsibility for their own employment opportunities and having that account, rather than doling out year after year more money from an unemployment system.

Q: Would you sign a bill to extend unemployment insurance if you were president right now?

A: If I were president right now, I would go to Congress with a new system for unemployment, which would have specific accounts from which people could withdraw their own funds. And I would not put in place a continuation of the current plan

Source: Iowa Straw Poll debate in Ames Iowa, Aug. 11, 2011

Gingrich on Unemployment

Go to college instead of 99 weeks of unemployment

Q: You criticized extending unemployment benefits, saying that you were "opposed to giving people money for doing nothing." Benefits have already been extended to 99 weeks, and they are set to expire soon. Would you extend unemployment benefits?

GINGRICH: I think unemployment compensation should be tied directly to a training program. And if you don't have a job and you need help, then in order for us to give you the help, you should sign up for a business-led training program so that that 99 weeks becomes an investment in human capital, so you can get a job. But I believe it is fundamentally wrong to give people money for 99 weeks for doing nothing. That's why we had welfare reform. If the president sends up a proposed extension, [Congress should] allow all 50 states to experiment with developing a mandatory training component of unemployment compensation. But I believe deeply, people should not get money for doing nothing.

Source: GOP Google debate in Orlando FL, Sept. 22, 2011

Fundamentally wrong to give unemployment pay for 99 weeks

We need to fundamentally change unemployment compensation. We need to require training. 99 weeks of unemployment sitting doing nothing could be turned into an associate's degree. I think that each state needs to have primary responsibility for most of these domestic issues.

Source: Head-to-head debate between Herman Cain & Newt Gingrich, Nov 5, 2011

Romney on Social Security Privatization

Favors private accounts; prepared to be entirely bold

Romney said he "was prepared to be entirely bold," in taking on the politically perilous issue of entitlement spending, "but I'm not prepared to cut benefits for low-income Americans." He said he favored private accounts and would consider tying Social Security benefits to prices rather than wages for higher income Americans.

Source: Bloomberg.com report on GOP primary debate in Orlando,
Oct. 21, 2007

Private accounts work better than extending retirement age

Currently, we're taking more money into Social Security that we actually send out. For people 20 and 30 and 40 years old, we have four major options for Social Security.

- The one Democrats want: raise taxes. It's the wrong way.

- The president said let's have private accounts and take that surplus money that's being gathered now in Social Security and put that into private accounts. That works.

- Other people said, well, extend the retirement age. That mathematically works. It's not as attractive.

- And the last is to index the Social Security benefits to something other than wages. But, in my view, that's the wrong way to go, other than for higher-income Americans. Let's consider indexing based on prices rather than wages.

Source: GOP primary debate in Orlando, Florida, Oct. 21, 2007

Gingrich on Social Security Privatization

Take Social Security off federal budget; give young a choice

You deal with Social Security as a free-standing issue. And the fact is, if you allow younger Americans to have the choice to go to a Galveston or Chilean-style personal Social Security savings account, the long-term effect on Social Security is scored by the Social Security actuary as absolutely stabilizing the system and taking care of it.

The key is there is $2.4 trillion in Social Security which should be off budget, and no president of the United States should ever again say because of some political fight in Washington, I may not be able to send you your check. That money is sitting there. That money is available. And the country ought to pay the debt it owes the people who put the money in there.

Source: CNBC GOP Primary debate in Rochester Michigan,
Nov. 9, 2011

Romney on Death Tax

Death tax just doesn't make sense

• Just say No: "I said no to a tax hike; raising taxes hurts working people and scares away jobs. I also said no to more borrowing; borrowing just shifts our problems to the backs of our kids. Instead, I went after waste, inefficiency, duplication, and patronage."

• The Death Tax: "It doesn't make sense to me that people get taxed when they can earn their money, get taxed when they save their money, and get taxed when they die. We should get rid of the death tax."

Source: The Man, His Values, & His Vision, p.115, Aug. 31, 2007

NOTE: The "Estate Tax" or "Inheritance Tax" is called the "Death Tax" by its opponents, beginning in 2001 under President Bush. While polls indicate broad support for eliminating the estate tax, few Americans are directly affected by it. Opponents point out that some family businesses would have to sold to pay the estate tax. In 2001, 98% of descendants avoid taxes altogether because the first $675,000 of an estate was exempt from taxation. That exemption rose to $5 million in 2011-2012, with a one-year repeal in 2010, and is slated to return to $1 million in 2013. According to the Internal Revenue Service, about 3,000 estates are worth more than $5 million each and hence would be subject to the tax in 2011-2012.

Gingrich on Death Tax

Death tax is a direct assault on civil society

Expansive government rapidly becomes expensive government, and that requires new and higher taxes. The transfer of money from citizens to the bureaucracy then further weakens civil society & leads to even more expensive & even more expensive government. That effort to finance Big Government through higher taxes is a direct assault on civil society, and the "death tax" is a prime example. This tax, which is in a constant state of flux and was resurrected in 2001 after effectively disappearing in 2010, falls especially hard on small business. That sector contributes immensely to America's social and economic dynamism, often acting as the cornerstone of community organizations and local philanthropy. Entrepreneurs and shopkeepers are community leaders and, when prosperous, are generous with their time and money. Prosperity and generosity are highly correlated, as those with more to give feel obliged to give more.

Source: A Nation Like No Other, by Newt Gingrich, pp.129-30,
Jun 13, 2011

Repeal tax hikes in capital gains and death taxes

Gingrich signed the Contract From America, clause 10:

Stop the Tax Hikes: Permanently repeal all tax hikes, including those to the income, capital gains, and death taxes, currently scheduled to begin in 2011.

Source: The Contract From America on July 8, 2010

Romney on Income Tax

Reduce the tax burden on middle-income families

I don't stay awake at night worrying about the taxes that rich people are paying. I'm concerned about the taxes that middle class families are paying. They're under a lot of pressure. Gasoline's expensive. Home heating oil, particularly in the Northeast, is very difficult for folks. Health care costs are going through the roof. Education costs and higher education are overwhelming. And as a result, we need to reduce the burden on middle-income families in this country.

Source: Des Moines Register Republican Debate, Dec. 12, 2007

Gingrich on Income Tax

Adopt a single-rate tax system

Gingrich signed the Contract From America, clause 4:

Enact Fundamental Tax Reform: Adopt a simple and fair single-rate tax system by scrapping the internal revenue code and replacing it with one that is no longer than 4,543 words—the length of the original Constitution.

Source: The Contract From America on July 8, 2010

Flat tax proposal criticized for losing popular tax breaks

Four out of five Americans would like to have the option of a one-page tax form with a single tax rate. This concept of an optional flat tax rate was developed by Steve Forbes when his flat tax campaign was undermined by criticisms that it would take away popular tax breaks. Forbes proposed giving American taxpayers an opportunity to choose simplicity versus complexity and a single rate over a lot of deductions. They call it the free choice flat tax, and it's an idea whose time has come.

All workers and corporations would have the freedom to choose each year to file their income taxes either under the new free choice flat tax option or under the current US income tax code.

Rhode Island adopted an optional flat tax, and lawmakers there expect that it will make the state more competitive with neighboring states in attracting new business and entrepreneurs who create jobs.

Source: Real Change, by Newt Gingrich, pp.143-4, Dec. 18, 2007

Romney vs. Gingrich on Social Issues

Social issues focus on matters which are based primarily on moral values. The GOP primaries make it sound like Romney and Gingrich differ substantially on these issues, but in reality they differ on focus rather than on substance, such as in the following topics:

- *Abortion:* including stem cells, partial birth, and state-level restrictions. This topic has always been the most viewed topic on our website www.OnTheIssues.org. Romney is anti-stem-cell and pro-life, but makes numerous exceptions; Gingrich makes fewer exceptions and more moral arguments.

- *Civil Rights:* including gay rights and minority rights. While Romney was governor of Massachusetts, his state's supreme court passed the nation's first same-sex marriage law. Romney is moderate on affirmative action. Gingrich authored DOMA, the Defense of Marriage Act, and agrees with Romney's opposition.

- *Education:* including college funding issues, school vouchers, and school prayer. Romney and Gingrich disagree on school prayer and the Department of Education; but mostly agree on vouchers.

- *Families and Children:* including father's rights and family values. Both Romney and Gingrich support family values but it's not a key focus for either candidate.

- *Principles and Values:* including religious issues and party issues. We cite opinions on the Tea Party, conservative values, religious values. The GOP primary focuses heavily on all three of those issues, but Gingrich and Romney focus even more heavily on "American Exceptionalism;" both wrote books on that subject.

- *Welfare and Poverty:* including homelessness, welfare payments, and other poverty programs. Romney and Gingrich agree that welfare causes dependency.

Mitt Romney
on Social Issues

Newt Gingrich
on Social Issues

Romney on Federal Abortion Laws

Would be delighted to sign federal ban on all abortions

Q: If hypothetically, *Roe v. Wade* was overturned, and the Congress passed a federal ban on all abortions and it came to your desk, would you sign it?

A: Let me say it. I'd be delighted to sign that bill. But that's not where we are. That's not where America is today. Where America is, is ready to overturn *Roe v. Wade* and return to the states that authority. But if the Congress got there, we had that kind of consensus in that country, terrific.

Source: GOP YouTube debate in St. Petersburg, Florida,
Nov. 28, 2007

NOTE: "*Roe v. Wade*" refers to the 1973 Supreme Court decision legalizing abortion. The essence of the Roe decision is that Constitutional rights apply only after birth; hence abortion does not breach a person's right to life. States cannot regulate 1st trimester abortions; states can regulate but not ban 2nd trimester abortions; and states can ban 3rd trimester abortions (as many have).

Gingrich on Federal Abortion Laws

Stop forcing pro-choice morality
on religious organizations

The campaign against public prayer and the display of religious symbols is only the tip of the iceberg. Consider the following examples:

- In May 2009, a pro-life nurse at a New York hospital was forced to participate in a late-term abortion, even though the hospital had agreed in writing to honor her religious convictions.

- In Jan. 2010, a Baptist minister was sentenced to thirty days in jail for peacefully protesting outside a Planned Parenthood abortion clinic in Oakland, California.

- In Feb. 2010, five men were threatened with arrest for preaching Christianity on a public sidewalk in Virginia.

The Founders would have regarded such efforts to remove God from public life as a fundamental threat to liberty. They saw no contradiction between the First Amendment, which was designed to *protect* religious liberty, and the need for a free people to remember that their liberties come from God.

Source: A Nation Like No Other, by Newt Gingrich, p. 87–89,
June 13, 2011

Romney on Stem Cells

Stem cell research lofty goals don't justify destroying life

Romney adopted the "pro-life" label after his battle over stem cell research. Ann Romney has multiple sclerosis. Romney, who not surprisingly cites the diagnosis of his wife's disease as one of the greatest blows of his life, is nevertheless alarmed by the aggressive program of embryonic stem cell research consortiums. He has taken a stand against the Harvard Stem Cell Institute.

The Harvard Stem Cell Institute was seeking legal protection for an embryo production line for the purpose of creating and harvesting stem cells, and Romney refused his support. He said, "Lofty goals do not justify the creation of life for experimentation or destruction."

Romney's views would permit for research the use of embryos about to be destroyed by their parents; this puts him at odds with President Bush's more restrictive position. Romney has never supported state-funded research on embryonic stem cells, and is a believer in the efficacy of alternative methods of producing stem cells.

Source: A Mormon in the White House?, by Hugh Hewitt, pp.111–4,
Mar. 12, 2007

Gingrich on Stem Cells

Embryonic stem-cell research desensitizes us to killing babies

Gingrich is drawing an increasingly hard line against the use of embryonic stem-cell research—a position that contrasts with statements that Gingrich himself has made on the subject in the past. Speaking at a Baptist church, the former speaker received a standing ovation when he declared that embryonic stem-cell research amounts to "the use of science to desensitize society over the killing of babies." And in a news conference, he said he would ban all embryonic stem-cell research, including that done on discarded embryos created by in vitro fertilization.

Social conservatives oppose embryonic stem cell research because it destroys days-old human embryos.

In contrast, in a news conference in July 2001, Gingrich said: "I think that there are ways to have appreciation for life, to recognize the sanctity of life, but nonetheless to look at fertility clinics where there are cells that are sitting there that are not going to be used to create life. They literally today, they're unregulated, they can be thrown away. And I think the president, I hope the president, will find a way to agree that there ought to be federally funded research."

Source: Karen Tumulty in Washington Post, "Vows Ban," Jan. 29, 2012

NOTES: Stem Cells are undifferentiated cells, which are useful in disease research. Stem cells are best taken from human fetuses; hence the pro-life opposition. Many pro-life advocates support fetal stem cell research because of the medical potential. In 2001, Pres. Bush announced that the federal policy would be to allow fetal stem cell research on existing stem cell lines but not on new ones.

Romney on Judicial Activism

Firmly pro-life; including Court nominations

Q: [to Santorum]: You are staunchly pro-life. Gov. Romney used to support abortion rights until he changed his position on this a few years ago. Should this be an issue in this primary campaign?

SANTORUM: I think an issue should be looking at the authenticity of that candidate and looking at their record over time and what they fought for. You can look at my record. A lot of folks run for president as pro-life and then that issue gets shoved to the back burner. The issue of pro-life, and the dignity of people at the end of life, those issues will be top priority issues for me to make sure that all life is respected and held with dignity.

ROMNEY: People have had a chance to look at my record and look what I've said. I believe people understand that I'm firmly pro-life. I will support justices who believe in following the Constitution and not legislating from the bench. And I believe in the sanctity of life from the very beginning until the very end.

Source: GOP primary debate in Manchester NH, June 13, 2011

Gingrich on Judicial Activism

Impeach judges who don't abide by Constitution as written

There is a sense of defeatism when it comes to the federal courts because the Left-liberal media insist on judicial supremacy and assert that the only way to check and balance the courts is to pass a constitutional amendment. This is of course absurd and historically wrong. The amendment process was not intended to be the way to check and balance Supreme Court decisions. There are some steps we can take through the legislative and executive branches to reestablish a constitutional balance.

1. The American people can insist on electing Senators who promise to confirm judges who enforce the Constitution as written.

2. The legislative & executive branches can limit jurisdiction of the federal courts to hear certain types of cases where they believe the federal judiciary is wrong.

3. Americans can only insist that judges who consistently ignore the Constitution and the legitimate powers of the other two coequal branches of the federal government be considered unfit the serve and be impeached.

Source: Winning the Future, by Newt Gingrich, pp. 81–4, Oct. 1, 2005

Romney on Welfare State

Opportunity is in our DNA;
dependency is death to initiative

What is it about American culture that has led us to become the most powerful nation in the history of the world? We believe in hard work and education. We love opportunity: almost all of us are immigrants or descendants of immigrants who came here for opportunity—opportunity is in our DNA. Americans love God, and those who don't have faith, typically believe in something greater than themselves. The values and beliefs of the free American people are the source of our nation's strength and they always will be.

The threat to our culture comes from within. The 1960's welfare programs created a culture of poverty. Some think we won that battle when we reformed welfare, but the liberals haven't given up. At every turn, they try to substitute government largesse for individual responsibility. Dependency is death to initiative, risk-taking and opportunity. Dependency is a culture-killing drug. We have got to fight it like the poison it is.

Source: Speech to 2008 Conservative Political Action Conference,
Feb. 7, 2008

Gingrich on Welfare State

When free welfare is provided, people choose not to work

President Lyndon Johnson famously announced the War on Poverty. From 1965 to 2008, total spending on this "war" reached nearly $16 trillion in 2008 dollars. And what did we get in return? Soon after the War on Poverty programs were adopted, the years-long decline in American poverty suddenly stopped.

By 2009 the poverty rate stood at 14.3%—about where it was when the War of Poverty began. With the government providing so much in free welfare, many people chose not to work. Welfare recipients who go to work lose their benefits as their income rises. This is effectively an extra tax on work that must be paid on top of the usual array of federal, state, and local taxes.

Source: A Nation Like No Other, by Newt Gingrich, p.109, June 13, 2011

FactCheck: Poverty rate has fallen under War on Poverty

PolitiFact.com reports: [LBJ's programs] focused on elderly poverty, which is down to 13%. [Gingrich also] uses the wrong numbers. The poverty rate was 17.3% in 1965, not 14%. So the poverty has fallen by 3 percentage points, or by about 1/6 its original level. Counting different years shows even more decline. In 1962, the poverty rate ranged was 20%. In pre-recession 2007, it stood at 12.5%. Comparing 1962 and 2007, the poverty rate dropped by over 1/3.

Source: FactCheck by PolitiFact.com, July 26, 2011

Romney on Don't-Ask-Don't-Tell

Don't ask, don't tell: sounds silly, but it's effective

Q: In 1994 you were quoted as saying that you advocated gays being able to serve openly and honestly in our nation's military. Do you still feel that way?

ROMNEY: No, actually, when I first heard of the "Don't ask, don't tell" policy, I thought it sounded awfully silly. I didn't think that would be very effective. And I turned out to be wrong. It's been the policy now in the military for what, 10, 15 years, and it seems to be working. This is not the time to put in place a major change, a social experiment, in the middle of a war going on. I wouldn't change it at this point. We can look at down the road. But it does seem to me that we have much bigger issues as a nation we ought to be talking about than that policy right now.

McCAIN: I think it would be a terrific mistake to even reopen the issue. The policy is working. And I am convinced that that's the way we can maintain this greatest military. Let's not tamper with them.

Source: GOP debate at Saint Anselm College, June 3, 2007

Gingrich on Don't-Ask-Don't-Tell

Army & Marines wanted Don't-Ask-Don't-Tell

Q: Now gays are allowed to serve openly in the military; would you leave that policy in place or would you try to change it back to "don't ask/don't tell"?

CAIN: If I had my druthers, I never would have overturned "don't ask/don't tell" in the first place. Now that they have changed it, I wouldn't create a distraction trying to turn it over as president.

GINGRICH: Well, I think it's very powerful that both the Army and the Marines overwhelmingly opposed changing it, that their recommendation was against changing it. And if as president—I've met with them and they said, you know, it isn't working, it is dangerous, it's disrupting unit morale, and we should go back, I would listen to the commanders whose lives are at risk about the young men and women that they are, in fact, trying to protect.

BACHMANN: I would keep the "don't ask/don't tell" policy.

Source: GOP primary debate in Manchester NH, June 13, 2011

NOTE: The policy banning open homosexuals serving in the military was repealed on Sept. 20, 2011. Hence gay and lesbian people may now openly serve in the US military. Since 1993, the DADT policy held that homosexuals may serve as long as they do not announce their homosexuality ("Don't Tell"), but also that the military may not investigate their homosexuality ("Don't Ask").

Romney on Defense of Marriage Act

MA Constitution, by John Adams, has no same-sex marriage

I've been in a state that has gay marriage, and I recognize that the consequences of gay marriage fall far beyond just the relationship between a man and a woman. They also relate to our kids and the right of religion to be practiced freely in a society.

The status of marriage, if it's allowed among the same sex individuals in one state is going to spread to the entire nation. And that's why it's important to have a national standard for marriage. And I'm committed to making sure that we reinforce the institution of marriage in this country by insisting that all states have a right to have marriage as defined as between a man and a woman; and we don't have unelected judges saying we're going to impose same-sex marriage where it was clearly not in their state constitution.

My state's constitution was written by John Adams. It isn't there. I've looked. The people need to speak on this issue and make sure that marriage is preserved as between a man and a woman.

Source: GOP primary debate in Orlando, Florida, Oct. 21, 2007

NOTE: "DOMA" refers to the Defense of Marriage Act, passed by Congress in 1996, which defined marriage as consisting of one man and one woman (in other words, barring same-sex marriage). DOMA applies to all federal benefits and taxes, but not necessarily to state benefits and taxes.

Gingrich on Defense of Marriage Act

I helped author DOMA; if it fails, amend Constitution

Q: Are you a George W. Bush Republican, meaning a constitutional amendment to ban same-sex marriage, or a Dick Cheney Republican, that same sex marriage should be a state's decision?

GINGRICH: I helped author the Defense of Marriage Act which the Obama administration should be protecting in court. I think if that fails, you have no choice except a constitutional amendment.

SANTORUM: Constitutional amendment.

PAWLENTY: Constitutional amendment.

CAIN: State decision.

ROMNEY: Constitutional.

Source: GOP primary debate in Manchester NH, June 13, 2011

Romney on Affirmative Action

Failure to educate minorities is a civil rights issue

The "achievement gap" has been lamented for decades but distressingly little has been done to combat it. About half of African American and Hispanic American students drop out before receiving a high-school degree. The result is that we are virtually assuring the creation of permanent underclass. It is an inexplicable human tragedy when millions of American children barely attain a third-world education in a nation that offers all its citizens access to free public schooling. Our current failure to educate our minority populations is the foremost civil-rights issue of our generation.

The minority proportion of the US population is projected to rise from 26% today to 34% by 2030, and if the achievement gap and dropout rate among minorities continues, the average educational level of the nation's entire workforce will continue to decline dramatically.

Source: No Apology, by Mitt Romney, pp.198-9, March 2, 2010

To compete as a nation, draw on skills of women & minorities

Women that I have seen in organizations have not had the opportunity that they deserve to have in getting ahead in organizations. If we are to compete as a nation, we've got to draw on the skills of women and minorities. And I have seen organizations from the federal government to corporations that are not drawing on the skills of women and minorities.

Source: MA Senate Debate with Ted Kennedy, Oct. 1, 1994

Gingrich on Affirmative Action

Affirmative action OK individually, but not by group

In 1995, a California referendum [was proposed to] eliminate affirmative action programs in state and local government. When Gingrich was asked about the issue at his regular daily press conference, he was consistent.

"It is my belief," he said, "that affirmative action programs, if done for individuals, are good, and if done by some group distinction, are bad. Because it is antithetical to the American dream to measure people by the genetic pattern of their great-grandmothers. So, I'm very interested in rewriting the affirmative action programs so that they allow individuals to get help whether they are Appalachian white or blacks from Atlanta. But I think it ought to be based on the fact that you individually have worked hard and are trying to rise and that you come out of a background of poverty and a background of cultural need."

A reporter noted that some beneficiaries of government preferences have been subjected to discrimination for centuries. "That's been true of virtually every American."

Source: Newt!, by Dick Williams, p. 31, June 1, 1995

Romney on College Loans

China and India graduate
more science and engineering PhDs

Increasing productivity begins with innovation and innovation begins with good ideas. More often than not, good ideas come from educated minds. America's post-WWII commitment to public higher education directly contributed to the burst of productivity that rocketed our economy beyond every other. But other nations have made as great or greater a commitment to higher education than we have, particularly in engineering, computer science, and information. 15 years ago, China and India awarded about half as many master's degrees in these fields as did the US. Today, they graduate more than two times the number of students in these fields as we do.

While our annual number of degrees has hovered around 7,000 to 8,000, China's has risen from 1,784 to 12,130—50% greater than ours. This is a stunning reversal of global preeminence in the priority attached to the highest level of educational attainment. Not surprisingly, China, Japan, and Taiwan claim a growing share of the world's patents.

Source: No Apology, by Mitt Romney, p.120, March 2, 2010

Gingrich on College Loans

College students should work and graduate with no debt

Rep. RON PAUL: [to Gingrich]: There's no authority in the Constitution for the federal government to be dealing with education. We should get rid of the student loan programs.

GINGRICH: The student loan program began when Lyndon Johnson announced it, I think, with a $15 million program. It's an absurdity. What does it do? It expands the ability of students to stay in college longer because they don't see the cost. It actually means they take fewer hours per semester on average. It takes longer for them to get through school. It allows them to tolerate tuitions going up absurdly.

Now, let me give you a contrast that's very startling. The College of the Ozarks is a work-study college. You have to work 20 hours a week during the year to pay tuition and books. Now, that is a model so different, it will be culture shock for the students of America to learn we actually expect them to go to class, study, get out quickly, charge as little as possible, and emerge debt free by doing the right things for 4 years.

Source: CNBC GOP Primary debate in Rochester MI, Nov. 9, 2011

Romney on School Vouchers

Supported means-tested vouchers
for public & private schools

- Pledged to vote to establish a means-tested school voucher program to allow students to attend the public or private school of their choice.

- Supported abolishing the federal Department of Education

- Favored keeping control of educational reform at the lowest level, closest to parents, teachers, and the community.

Source: Boston Globe review of 1994 campaign issues, Mar. 21, 2002

School choice over fat-cat CEOs of teachers' unions

Our conservative agenda strengthens our family in part by, by putting our schools on track to be the best in the world again, because great schools start with great teachers. We'll insist on hiring teachers from the top third college graduates and we'll give better teachers better pay. School accountability, school choice, cyber schools will be priorities and we'll put parents and teachers back in charge of education, not fat-cat CEOs of the teachers' unions.

Source: Speech to 2010 Conservative Political Action Conference,
Feb. 20, 2010

Gingrich on School Vouchers

Voucherize inner-city programs from schools to groceries

In a speech in March, 1995, to business leaders in suburban Atlanta, Gingrich noted that the public school system in the District of Columbia spends $9,600 a year per pupil, nearly double the national average. He suggested that for such a high level of spending, each could have private tutors and personal transportation to school—plus lunch. He advocates vouchers to parents so they can choose the schools, public or private, their children will attend.

"I think we ought to voucherize every program in the inner city with cash payments to parents allowing them to decide where and what to purchase, be it an elementary school, health care, or groceries." Some in his audience thought he was exaggerating to make a point. In a later interview, he was willing to go even further. "Suppose you need to get children away from failed teachers. What if we called on the home-schoolers in Maryland and Virginia to come to D.C. for a massive home schooling program, teaching parents how to teach their children."

Source: Newt!, by Dick Williams, pp. 51-2, June 1, 1995

Romney on Department of Education

Changed from closing Education Dept. to supporting NCLB

Q: You have been criticized for changing your position on some issues. You say that it's a part of learning from experience. Can you point to an area in which your learning from experience led you to change to a position that is less popular with the Republican base?

A: Sure, quite a few, actually. One is No Child Left Behind. I've taken a position where, once upon a time, I said I wanted to eliminate the Department of Education. That was my position when I ran for Senate in 1994. That's very popular with the base. As I've been a governor and seen the impact that the federal government can have holding down the interest of the teachers' unions and instead putting the interests of the kids and the parents and the teachers first, I see that the Department of Education can actually make a difference. So I supported No Child Left Behind. I still do. I know there are a lot in my party that don't like it, but I like testing in our schools. I think it allows us to get better schools.

Source: Republican Debate in South Carolina, May 15, 2007

Gingrich on Department of Education

Dramatically shrink the federal Department of Education

Q: What as president would you seriously do about a massive overreach of big government into the classroom?

Gov. GARY JOHNSON: I am going to promise to advocate the abolishment of the federal Department of Education.

GINGRICH: I think you need very profound reform of education at the state level. You need to dramatically shrink the federal Department of Education, get rid of virtually all of its regulations. And the truth is, I believe we'd be far better off if most states adopted a program of the equivalent of Pell Grants for K-through-12, so that parents could choose where their child went to school, whether it was public, or private, or home-schooling, and parents could be involved. Florida has a virtual school program that is worth the entire country studying as an example

Source: GOP Google debate in Orlando FL, Sept. 22, 2011

Romney on School Prayer

Schools can teach family values,
but not religion or prayer

Romney said he would support federal grants to schools to fund programs stressing the importance of economics and family values. He said that local school districts should have complete control over the programs, but that they could not endorse specific religious beliefs or prayer in schools. Among the possible programs could be teaching children to learn the importance of getting married before having children.

Source: Joe Battenfeld in Boston Herald, Aug. 1, 1994

Gingrich on School Prayer

Voluntary school prayer creates bond between you and Creator

There's a reason why voluntary school prayer mattered, and the reason goes far from the concept of being endowed by our Creator and getting authority from a Supreme Being.

I had a very bright student in the class who said, "Do you really think voluntary school prayer matters that much? Why does it matter? You really think 30 seconds matter?" And I suddenly realized the reason it matters is it establishes at the beginning of the day the concept of a hierarchy. That the teacher is an intermediary between the Creator who is endowing is with our unalienable rights and us.

If there is a Creator and your rights are endowed by the Creator, then there is a direct bond between you and the Creator. Now this is not a violation of church and state. They're not teaching you to be a Catholic or to be Jewish or Muslim or Baptist or Methodist. They're teaching you basic principles of morality and basic principles of relating to personal strength as an act of faith in a Creator.

Source: Newt!, by Dick Williams, p.172-173, June 1, 1995

Romney on Fathers In Families

Child development enhanced by having a mother & father

The attack on faith & religion is no less relentless. Tolerance for pornography and sexual promiscuity, combined with the twisted incentives of government welfare programs have led to today's grim realities: 68% of African American children are born out-of-wedlock; 45% of Hispanic children; 25% of White children. How much harder it is for these children to succeed in school and in life. A nation built on the principles of the Founding Fathers cannot long stand when its children are raised without fathers in the home.

The development of a child is enhanced by having a mother and father. Such a family is the ideal for the future of the child and for the strength of a nation. I wonder how it is that unelected judges, like some in my state of Massachusetts, are so unaware of this reality, so oblivious to the millennia of recorded history. It is time for the people of America to fortify marriage through Constitutional amendment, so that liberal judges cannot continue to attack it.

Source: Speech to Conservative Political Action Conference,
Feb. 7, 2008

Gingrich on Fathers In Families

Responsibility for child's education resides with parents

Our public school system is increasingly geared toward serving the needs of government employee unions and other special interest groups instead of the educational, moral, and emotional needs of our children. With public schools becoming increasingly bureaucratic, hostile to religious expression, and unresponsive to parental input, American families are increasingly choosing alternative education methods for their children such as private schools, charter schools, and homeschooling. Such options allow parents to customize their child's curriculum and learning environment, provide a safe environment free of drugs and violence, and impart strong religious values.

The point is not to demonize the public school system. Rather, the point is to reinforce the time-honored principle that the authority and responsibility to raise children, direct their education, and instill in them the values that make a free society flourish, all reside with the child's parents, not the state.

Source: A Nation Like No Other, by Newt Gingrich, p. 95, June 13, 2011

Romney on the Tea Party

Me & Tea Party are both
for small government & low spending

Q: Are you a member of the Tea Party?

ROMNEY: I don't think you carry cards in the Tea Party. I believe in a lot of what the Tea Party believes in. The Tea Party believes that government's too big, and taxing too much. I put together a plan with a whole series of points of how we can get America's economy going again. Tea Party people like that. So if the Tea Party is for keeping government small and spending down, and helping us create jobs, then, hey, I'm for the Tea Party.

Source: GOP debate in Simi Valley CA at the Reagan Library,
Sept. 7, 2011

Gingrich on the Tea Party

Tea Party prevents mistake of
electing conservative Democrats

Q: What role do you think the Tea Party will play in the 2012 elections?

A: Tea Party will help prevent Republicans from making same mistakes of 2004 and 2006 & help elect conservative democrats. The most important role for the Tea Party is not in elections, but in developing local solutions as we move power out of Washington. Permanently ending the age of big government will be hard work and require a team effort between federal, state & local government.

Source: Republican primary debate on Twitter.com, July 21, 2011

Romney on Religious Values

Freedom requires religion just as religion requires freedom

Freedom requires religion just as religion requires freedom. Freedom opens the windows of the soul so that man can discover his most profound beliefs and commune with God. Freedom and religion endure together, or perish alone. Given our grand tradition of religious tolerance and liberty, some wonder whether there are any questions regarding an aspiring candidate's religion that are appropriate. I believe there are.

Source: Speech "Faith In America" at Bush Library, Dec. 6, 2007

Freedom requires religion in society, not in individuals

Q: Can you have freedom without organized religion?

A: John Adams said that our constitutional form of government in this nation would require morality and freedom to be able to survive. We believe, as a nation, that God gave the individual certain inalienable rights. That's not a constitutional guarantee, that's not a policy guarantee, it's a guarantee from our creator.

Q: Can you be a moral person and be an atheist?

A: Oh, of course.

Q: So freedom doesn't require religion?

A: Our constitutional form of government and this American experiment requires morality, which in turn required religion. Yet, of course, on an individual basis, you have many individuals of great morality that don't have any particular faith.

Source: Meet the Press: "Meet the Candidates" series, Dec. 16, 2007

Gingrich on Religious Values

Declaration assumes God created man

One of the Declaration's most famous passages proclaims, "All men are created equal, that they are endowed by their Creator with certain unalienable Rights...." This assertion makes some key assumptions about the relationship between man and God: It assumes that God created man. It assumes that man must obey an order of justice that God has instituted. That order of justice requires all men and women to honor each other's natural rights, because these rights are an unalienable endowment from the Almighty. When someone violates another's rights, he is not merely breaking the law, he is violating God's grant of protection.

Source: A Nation Like No Other, by Newt Gingrich, p. 21, June 13, 2011

Constitution says freedom *of* religion, not *from* religion

The Bill of Rights' Amendment 1 begins: "Congress shall make no law respecting an establishment of religion, or prohibiting the free exercise thereof."

The language clearly prohibits the establishment of an official national religion, while at the same time protecting the observance of religion in both private and public spaces. In fact, two of the principal authors of the First Amendment, Thomas Jefferson and James Madison, both attended church services in the Capitol building. Therefore, these Founding Fathers clearly saw no conflict in opposing the establishment of an official religion while protecting the freedom of religious expression in the public square.

Source: Rediscovering God in America, by Newt Gingrich, pp. 31-2,
Dec 31, 2006

Romney on American Exceptionalism

American Exceptionalism means America need not decline

In a world composed of nations that are filled with rage and hate for the US, our president should proudly defend her rather than continually apologize for her. I reject the view that America must decline. I believe in American exceptionalism. I am convinced that we can act together to strengthen the nation, to preserve our global leadership, and to protect freedom where it exits and promote it where it does not. What is ahead of us now will not be easy.

It will be difficult to overcome the challenges we face, to maintain our national strength and purpose even as China, Russia, and the jihadists pursue their own ambitions. It will be difficult to repair the damage from the economic panic of 2008 and the intemperate actions that have been justified as steps to remedy it. I don't worry about our ability to overcome any problem or threat. But I do wonder whether we will take this action that is timely, and that we will act before the necessary correction is massively disruptive.

Source: No Apology, by Mitt Romney, pp. 29&33, March 2, 2010

NOTE: "American exceptionalism" means that America has a unique status in the world today. The interest in American exceptionalism counters Obama's rejection of the concept, when Obama said, "Sure, I believe in American exceptionalism in the same way the British believe in British exceptionalism." Republicans generally interpret that as meaning, "No, I don't believe in your version of American exceptionalism at all."

Gingrich on American Exceptionalism

Five habits of liberty sustain American Exceptionalism

Looking through 400 years of American history, we find five habits of liberty that have been crucial to sustaining American Exceptionalism.

They are: faith and family, work, civil society, rule of law, and safety and peace.

Tempering man's worst impulses, these distinctly American habits are vital to cultivating an engaged, informed citizenry, which is needed to sustain a free republic and secure the unalienable rights asserted in the Declaration of Independence. The emphasis on these habits set America apart from its European counterparts, where monarchs were intent on cultivating passive, obedient subjects unlikely to change their ruler's claim to power.

Source: A Nation Like No Other, by Newt Gingrich, p. 42, June 13, 2011

Romney on Conservative Values

Obama's record: debt, decline, and disappointment

Tonight, the President will give a nice speech with a lot of memorable phrases. But he won't give you the hard numbers. Like $15 trillion—that's the size of our national debt.

Instead, tonight, President Obama will make the opening argument in his campaign against a "Do Nothing Congress." But for two years, this President had a Congress that could do everything he wanted.

Did he fix the economy? Did he tackle the housing crisis? Did he get Americans back to work? No.

- He spent $787 billion on a stimulus bill and put us on track to borrow and spend $5 trillion in just his first term.

- He forced through Obamacare—a trillion-dollar entitlement we can't afford.

- He took over auto companies and student loans.

- He's spearheaded one of the largest expansions of government in American history. And he's paying for it with money borrowed from China.

President Obama has amassed an actual record of debt, decline, and disappointment.

Source: Prebuttal to Obama's State of the Union speech, Jan. 24, 2012

Gingrich on Conservative Values

Liberals exploit weakness; conservatives offer strength

We must expect liberals to continue to fight us, and where they do so honestly, to respect them for it while continuing to work for our success. But it is well to remember that temptation is something ever lurking, waiting to exploit human weakness, especially in difficult times. What we have to offer people instead is strength and adventure, the experience of a new level of life-enhancing energy and love of a great country. We have no reason to become distressed—as many members of the House did and as I at some point also did. What we are embarked on is what they call steady work, more than enough for a lifetime.

Source: Lessons Learned the Hard Way, by Newt Gingrich, pp. 82-3, Jul 2, 1998

Red-blue split is 85% Americans and 15% fringe

The media tell us America is a nation divided between conservative red states and liberal blue states. They tell us that red and blue are equally divided—which is why elections are so close, and why Congress seems gridlocked.

But that's simply not true. The reality is the American people are united on almost every important issue facing our country. The real division is between red-white-blue America (about 85% of the country) and a fringe on the left (about 15% of the country). Not only have the media perpetuated the myth that the country is equally divided, but the elites on the left fringe have also insisted that their positions hold moral superiority. Neither is true.

Source: Real Change, by Newt Gingrich, p. 3, Dec. 18, 2007

Romney vs. Gingrich on International Issues

International issues focus on foreign relations and anything involving foreign nations. Romney and Gingrich once again agree on the basics and differ mostly in attitude ("Tough and Tougher"). They differ on immigration, but mostly agree on the following topics:

- *Energy and Oil:* including global warming, domestic drilling and alternative energy sources. Romney and Gingrich both want domestic oil drilling and both accept global warming but not on an international solution.

- *Free Trade:* including NAFTA (the North American Free Trade Agreement) and other bilateral agreements, plus opinions on the trade organizations like the WTO (World Trade Organization). Romney wants to push China; so does Gingrich; neither focuses on this issue.

- *Immigration:* including border security; the border fence; and dealing with the current 12 million illegal immigrants in the US. Romney popularizes the concept of "self-deportation"; Gingrich supports local "Citizen Boards" for deportation decisions.

- *Foreign Policy:* Gingrich and Romney both hint at military solutions in Iran and Cuba; both fear socialism and want to align US policy to avoid it.

- *Homeland Security:* This category includes defense spending issues and defense strategy goals. Gingrich and Romney both want dramatic increases in defense spending and no change in terrorism policy.

- *War and Peace:* including the current ongoing wars in Iraq and Afghanistan. Gingrich and Romney would both stay in Afghanistan; and both would have stayed in Iraq. Both strongly support Israel but differ on how to address the issue publicly.

Mitt Romney
on International Issues

Newt Gingrich
on International Issues

Romney on Climate Change

They don't call it "America warming" but "global warming"

When you put in place a new cap or a mandate, and particularly if you don't have any safety valve as to how much the cost of that cap might be, you would impose on the American people, if you do it unilaterally, without involving all the world, you'd impose on the American people a huge new effective tax: 20% on utilities, 50 cents a gallon for gasoline—that's according to the energy information agency—would be imposed on us. What happens if you do that? You put a big burden on energy in this country as the energy-intensive industries say, "We're going to move our new facilities from the US to China, where they don't have those agreements." You end up polluting and putting just as much CO_2 in the air because the big energy users go there. That's why these ideas make sense, but only on a global basis. They don't call it "America warming." They call it "global warming." That's why you've got to have a president that understands the real economy.

Source: Republican debate at Reagan Library in Simi Valley,
Jan. 30, 2008

NOTE: "Cap-and-Trade" refers to a carbon dioxide (CO_2) emissions policy where the amount of CO_2 is "capped" at a government-specified emission amount, and then the right to emit CO_2 is "traded" via emission permits. A similar program was used successfully to battle acid rain via sulfur dioxide emission permits trading on the Chicago Mercantile Exchange.

Gingrich on Climate Change

Kyoto treaty is bad for the environment and bad for America

Kyoto is a bad treaty. It is bad for the environment and it is bad for America. It sets standards that will require massive investments by the US but virtually no investments by other countries. The Senate was right when it voted unanimously against the treaty. We should insist on revisiting the entire Kyoto process and resolutely reject efforts to force us into an anti-American, environmentally failed treaty.

The US should support substantial research into climate science, managing the response to climate change, & in developing new non-carbon energy systems. It is astounding to watch people blithely propose trillions of dollars in spending on a topic on which we have failed to spend modest amounts to better understand.

It is astounding to have people focus myopically on carbon as the sole source of climate change. The world's climate has changed in the past with sudden speed and dramatic impact. Global warming may happen. On the other hand it is possible Europe will experience another ice age.

Source: Gingrich Communications website, www.newt.org, Dec. 1, 2006

NOTE: "Kyoto" refers to a Climate Change Treaty which sets carbon dioxide reduction targets for the US and other developed countries. Completed in 1998, the US has not yet signed. This is politically controversial because it would require the US to cut CO_2 emissions, which is potentially costly.

Romney on Oil Drilling

Develop alternative energy but also drill in ANWR

To remain the economic and military superpower, America must address achieving energy independence. We must become independent from foreign sources of oil. This will mean a combination of efforts related to conservation and efficiency measures, developing alternative sources of energy like biodiesel, ethanol, nuclear, and coal gasification, and finding more domestic sources of oil such as in ANWR or the Outer Continental Shelf (OCS).

Source: PAC website, www.TheCommonwealthPac.com, "Meet Mitt,"
Dec 1, 2006

NOTES: "ANWR" refers to the Arctic National Wildlife Refuge, a protected area in northern Alaska that contains substantial supplies of oil and gas. Conservatives favor drilling ANWR to extract the oil, while liberals favor maintaining its protected status.

"OCS" refers to drilling for oil off the Outer Continental Shelf, several miles offshore. States control oil drilling in waters up to three miles offshore; the federal government controls waters from that distance until the continental shelf ends and the deep ocean begins (a maximum of about 350 miles offshore). Conservatives favor OCS drilling to reach more potential oil reserves; liberals cite the greater technical challenges and the higher risk of oil spills.

Gingrich on Oil Drilling

2008 book: Drill Here, Drill Now, Pay Less

In 2008, American Solutions launched an online petition drive to demand Congress lift the 25-year-old moratorium on new offshore drilling. We collected 1.5 million signatures. Our effort sparked a nationwide grassroots rebellion that resulted in Congress allowing the moratorium to expire.

I wrote a book in fall 2008 called "Drill Here, Drill Now, Pay Less," describing America's vast energy potential and explain how misguided government policies have prevented us from becoming an energy powerhouse.

Source: Real Change, by Newt Gingrich, pp.205-6, Dec. 18, 2007

2008 petition drive: Drill here, Drill now, Pay less

In 2008 when gasoline was at $4 a gallon, American Solutions launched a petition drive: Drill here, Drill now, Pay less.

The Left couldn't survive in a world where we had the courage to say, "Why don't we find American oil and why don't we find American gas, and why don't we have the next building boom in the United States, not in Dubai. And why don't we make sure that the terrorists run out of money?" And that ought to be our approach to this, so let's do it now.

First of all: Reopen off of Louisiana. The people of Louisiana want it to happen. So let's reopen the areas off only those states that want to reopen them. Let's let them do it now.

Source: Speech at Conservative Political Action Conference, Feb. 11, 2011

Romney on China Trade

China doesn't want to have a trade war; so push hard

Q: Candidates have talked tough on China before—George W. Bush did it, Barack Obama did it—but once elected, the president takes a much more cautious approach.

A: They have been played like a fiddle by the Chinese. And the Chinese are smiling all the way to the bank, taking our currency and taking our jobs and taking a lot of our future. And I'm not willing to let that happen. We've got to call cheating for what it is.

Q: Isn't that risking a trade war?

A: Well, now, think about that. We buy this much stuff from China; they buy that much stuff from us. You think they want to have a trade war? This is a time when we're being hollowed out by China that is artificially holding down their prices. On day one, I will issue an executive order identifying China as a currency manipulator. We'll bring an action against them in front of the WTO for manipulating their currency. If you're not willing to stand up to China, you'll get run over by China. And that's what's happened for 20 years.

Source: GOP debate at Dartmouth College, NH, Oct. 11, 2011

NOTE: "WTO" refers to the World Trade Organization, an international organization intended to reduce trade barriers, formed in 1995. WTO members (which include China since 2001) charge minimal import tariffs on each other. The WTO adjudicates international disputes over trade barriers, such as currency manipulation.

Gingrich on China Trade

Protectionism helps China & India challenge US supremacy

In the US, there exists a coalition of union leaders who prefer protection over competition. This liberal coalition complains about companies' outsourcing jobs while insisting on corporate taxes that encourage companies to go overseas. They prefer that government impose on business obsolete, absurd work rules, even though these raise costs, lower productivity, and make America less competitive in the world market.

The challenge to American economic supremacy from 1.3 billion Chinese and more than 1.1 billion Indians is vastly greater than anything we have previously seen. India's embrace of capitalism and China's bizarre combination of Marxist-Leninist government and free market initiatives will create a future where one-fourth of the world's markets will be controlled by these countries. Those who advocate economic isolationism and protectionism are advocating a policy that could help China and India surpass the US in economic power in our children's or grandchildren's lifetime.

Source: Gingrich Communications website, www.newt.org, Dec. 1, 2006

Romney on Self-Deportation

Enforce employment laws;
illegal immigrants will self-deport

Q: [to Gingrich]: We heard from Gov. Romney, that self-deportation, or illegal immigrants leaving the country voluntarily, is a possible solution. You've suggested that self-deportation is "an Obama level fantasy."

GINGRICH: I actually agree that self-deportation will occur if you're single. I would just suggest that grandmothers or grandfathers aren't likely to self-deport.

ROMNEY: Those who come into the country legally would be given an identification card, and if employers hire someone without a card, then those employers would be severely sanctioned. If you do that, people who have come here illegally won't be able to find work. And over time, those people would tend to leave the country, or self-deport. I don't think anyone is interested in going around and rounding up people around the country and deporting 11 million illegal immigrants into America. Let's focus our attention on how to make legal immigration work and stop illegal immigration.

Source: CNN GOP primary debate on the eve of Florida primary,
Jan 26, 2012

Gingrich on Self-Deportation

Romney's "self-deportation" is an Obama-level fantasy

Q: You've suggested that self-deportation as advocated by Governor Romney is in your words, "An Obama-level fantasy." Why?

GINGRICH: First of all, you should control the border, which I have pledged to do by January 1, 2014. You should also make deportation easier so when you deport people who shouldn't be here. I actually agree that self-deportation will occur if you're single. If you've only been here a short time. And there are millions of people who faced with that, would go back home, file for a guest worker program and might or might not come back. People who have been here a very long time who are married, who may well have children and grandchildren. And I would just suggest that grandmothers or grandfathers aren't likely to self-deport. I offered a proposal, a citizen panel to review whether or not somebody who had been here a very long time, who had family and who had an American family willing to sponsor them, should be allowed to get residency, but not citizenship.

Source: CNN GOP primary debate on the eve of Florida primary,
Jan 26, 2012

Romney on Immigrant Policy

Turn off the magnet that attracts immigrants

I learned this when I was with border patrol agents in San Diego, and they said, look, they can always get a ladder to go over the fence. And people will always run to the country. The reason they come in such great numbers is because we've left the magnet on.

And I said, what do you mean, the magnet? And they said, when employers are willing to hire people who are here illegally, that's a magnet, and it draws them in. And sanctuary cities, giving tuition breaks to the kids of illegal aliens, employers that knowingly hire people who are here illegally. Those things also have to be stopped.

If we want to secure the border, we have to make sure we have a fence, determining where people are, enough agents to oversee it, & turn off that magnet. We can't talk about amnesty, we cannot give amnesty to those who have come here illegally.

We've got 4.7 million people waiting in line legally. Let those people come in first, and those that are here illegally, they shouldn't have a special deal.

Source: GOP debate in Simi Valley CA at the Reagan Library,
Sept. 7, 2011

Gingrich on Immigrant Policy

Review all illegal aliens & if you have no ties, go home

Q: Back in the '80s, you voted for legislation that had a pathway to citizenship for illegal immigrants. Some called it amnesty then; they still call it amnesty now. What would you do if you were President, with these millions of illegal immigrants, many of whom have been in this country for a long time?

GINGRICH: Let me start and just say I think that we ought to have an H-1 visa that goes with every graduate degree in math, science and engineering so that people stay here. I did vote for the Simpson-Mazzoli Act. I believe ultimately you have to find some system that reviews the people who are here. If you've come here recently, you have no ties to this country, you ought to go home. If you've been here 25 years and you got three kids and two grandkids, you've been paying taxes and obeying the law, you belong to a local church, I don't think we're going to separate you from your family, uproot you forcefully and kick you out.

Source: CNN National Security GOP primary debate, Nov. 22, 2011

NOTE: The "Simpson-Mazzoli Act" refers to the Immigration Reform and Control Act of 1986, was the immigration reform supported by President Reagan. Its opponents claimed that it granted amnesty in exchange for tightening immigration law, but that the tightening never occurred while the amnesty did.

Romney on Guest Workers

I like legal immigration; let business determine visas

Q: In 2008, you said you favored allowing American companies to hire more skilled foreign workers. With unemployment at 9.1%, are you still for importing more foreign labor?

A: Well, of course not. We're not looking to bring people in for jobs that can be done by Americans. But at the same time, we want to make sure that America welcomes the best and brightest in the world. If someone comes here and gets a PhD in physics, that's the person I'd like to staple a green card to their diploma, rather than saying to them to go home. I want the best & brightest to be metered into the country based upon the needs of our employment sector & create jobs by bringing technology and innovation that comes from people around the world. I like legal immigration I'd have the number of visas that we give to people here that come here legally, determined in part by the needs of our employment community. But we have to secure our border and crack down on those that bring folks here and hire here illegally.

Source: Iowa Straw Poll GOP debate in Ames Iowa, Aug. 11, 2011

Gingrich on Guest Workers

I voted for Reagan's legal guest worker program

Q: Your current perception on immigration reform is a little different on your initial positions under Reagan?

GINGRICH: I think we have to find a way to get to a country in which everybody who's here is here legally. But you referenced President Reagan. In 1986, I voted for the Simpson-Mazzoli Act, which in fact did grant some amnesty in return for promises. President Reagan wrote in his diary that year that he signed the act because we were going to control the border and we were going to have an employer program where it was a legal guest worker program. That's in his diary. I'm with President Reagan. We ought to control the border, we ought to have a legal guest worker program. We ought to outsource it, frankly, to American Express, Visa, and MasterCard, so there's no counterfeiting, which there will be with the federal government. We should be very tough on employers once you have that legal program.

Source: GOP debate in Simi Valley CA at the Reagan Library,
Sept. 7, 2011

Romney on Official English

English should be the official language of the US

Q: Governor, you had an ad running saying that Speaker Gingrich called Spanish "the language of the ghetto." What do you mean by that?

ROMNEY: [to Gingrich]: Did you say that?

GINGRICH: No. What I said was, we want everybody to learn English. I didn't use the word "Spanish." We do not want anyone trapped in a situation where they cannot get a job, they cannot rise. And that's why I think English should be the official language of government, and that's why I think every young American should learn English.

ROMNEY: I think our position on English in our schools and in our nation is the same, which I believe English should be the official language of the United States. I also believe that in our schools, we should teach kids in English. I fought for a program to have English immersion in our schools so our kids could learn in English. I think we agree on this: Kids in this country should learn English so they can have all the jobs and all the opportunity of people who are here.

Source: CNN GOP primary debate on the eve of Florida primary,
Jan 26, 2012

Gingrich on Official English

Require official English plus American history

We should make English the official language of government. We should insist that first-generation immigrants who come here learn American history in order to become citizens. And then find a way to deal with folks who are already here, some of whom, frankly, have been here 25 years, are married with kids, live in our local neighborhood, go to our church. It's got to be done in a much more humane way than thinking that to automatically deport millions of people

Source: GOP debate in Simi Valley CA at the Reagan Library,
Sept. 7, 2011

NOTE: Anti-immigration advocates often seek Official English status (the US has no official language), which would enforce assimilation of non-English speaking immigrants. Similarly, anti-immigration advocates seek to terminate Bilingual Education, which is currently funded in school systems with large non-English-speaking populations.

Romney on Cuba Policy

Free Cuba and eliminate threat
of people like Hugo Chavez

Q: Cuban dictatorship has survived nine US presidents. What would you do differently?

A: You've got to think about who Fidel Castro is, and who Raul Castro is as well. We call them strongmen—dictators, totalitarian leaders. And yet these are individuals who are not strong. Look at what they have done: People wearing a wristband that says "change" are arrested—25 of them just for wearing a wristband. These Castro brothers are cowards, and we have to recognize they are cowards. And for that reason, the course for America is to continue our isolation of Cuba. It is not to say, as Barack Obama on the Democratic side said, that he would dignify the Castros with a personal visit to Cuba. That's not the way to go. Instead, it's to bring our friends together to isolate Cuba, to put together a strategy that helps all of Latin America, weakens Hugo Chavez who is propping up Castro. We need a Latin American policy that frees Cuba and that eliminates a threat of people like Hugo Chavez.

Source: Republican primary debate on Univision, Dec. 9, 2007

Gingrich on Cuba Policy

I supported Helms-Burton to isolate the Castro regime

ROMNEY: [to Gingrich] The right course for Cuba is to continue to honor Helms-Burton. I will use every resource we have, short of invasion and military action, to make sure that when Fidel Castro finally leaves this planet, that we are able to help the people of Cuba enjoy freedom.

GINGRICH: I was very proud as Speaker to be able to make sure that the Helms-Burton Act passed, and I'm delighted that Rep. Dan Burton is campaigning with me, because it was a very important step towards isolating the Castro regime. We should facilitate the transition from dictatorship to freedom. We want to bring together every non-military asset we have, exactly as Pres. Reagan did in Eastern Europe: he broke up the Soviet empire without a general war by using a wide range of things, one of which is just psychological, saying to the next generation of people in Cuba, the dictatorship is not going to survive. You need to bet on freedom & prosperity in Cuba, and we will help you get to that freedom.

Source: CNN GOP primary debate in Florida, Jan. 26, 2012

NOTE: "Helms-Burton" refers to the Cuban Liberty and Democratic Solidarity Act of 1996, sponsored by Sen. Jesse Helms (R, NC) and Rep. Dan Burton (R, IN). The law extended the embargo against Cuba, initiated by Pres. Eisenhower in 1960 and strengthened by Pres. Kennedy in 1962. The embargo expresses US opposition to Fidel Castro's communist policies in Cuba. Fidel Castro retired in 2008; the Communist Party still rules via Fidel's brother Raul Castro. Pres. Obama has promised to relax the embargo but as of 2012, only the travel ban was slightly loosened.

Romney on Iranian Sanctions

Unacceptable for Iran to become a nuclear nation

Q: How would you approach the new reality for our ally, Israel, and the existential threats it faces from Iran, Hamas, and Hezbollah?

ROMNEY: Very simple. You start off by saying that you don't allow an inch of space to exist between you and your friends and your allies. The president went about this all wrong. He went around the world and apologized for America. He addressed the United Nations in his inaugural address and chastised our friend, Israel, for building settlements and said nothing about Hamas launching thousands of rockets into Israel.

The right course for us is to stand behind our friends, to listen to them, and to let the entire world know that we will stay with them and that we will support them and defend them. And with regards to Iran, which perhaps represents the greatest existential threat to Israel, we have to make it abundantly clear: It is unacceptable—and I take that word carefully—it is unacceptable for Iran to become a nuclear nation.

Source: GOP Google debate in Orlando FL, Sept. 22, 2011

Gingrich on Iranian Sanctions

Sabotage Iran's oil refinery

PERRY: [to Gingrich]: We need to sanction the Iranian Central Bank. That will shut down that economy.

GINGRICH: We ought to have a massive all-sources energy program, designed to literally replace the Iranian oil. Now that's how we won World War II. We all get sucked into these tactical discussions. We need a strategy of defeating and replacing the current Iranian regime with minimum use of force. But if we were serious, we could break the Iranian regime, I think, within a year, starting candidly with cutting off the gasoline supply to Iran, and then, frankly, sabotaging the only refinery they have.

Q: But sanctions on the Iranian Central Bank now, is that a good idea or a bad idea?

GINGRICH: I think it's a good idea if you're serious about stopping them. I think replacing the regime before they get a nuclear weapon without a war beats replacing the regime with war, which beats allowing them to have a nuclear weapon. Those are your three choices.

Source: CNN National Security GOP primary debate Nov. 22, 2011

Romney on Israel/Palestine

Disagree with Israelis in private; stand with them in public

Q: Do you agree with Speaker Gingrich that the Palestinians "an invented people"?

ROMNEY: I happen to agree with most of what the speaker said, except by going down and saying the Palestinians are an invented people. That I think was a mistake on the speaker's part. I think the speaker would probably suggest that as well.

GINGRICH: No.

ROMNEY: Israel does not want us to make it more difficult for them to sit down with the Palestinians. Ultimately, the Palestinians and the Israelis are going to have to agree on how they're going to settle the differences between them. My view is this: We stand with the Israeli people. We link arms with them. If we disagree with them, like this president has time and time again, we don't do it in public like he's done it, we do it in private. And we let the Israeli leadership describe what they believe the right course is going forward.

Source: Yahoo's "Your Voice Your Vote" debate in Iowa, Dec. 10, 2011

Gingrich on Israel/Palestine

Tell the truth: Palestinians are an "invented people"

Q: You caused a stir in the Middle East by calling the Palestinians "an invented people." The chief Palestinian negotiator said, "These statements of Gingrich will be the ammunition of the bin Ladens and the extremists for a long, long time."

GINGRICH: How would he know the difference? Look, is what I said factually correct? Yes. Is it historically true? Yes. Are we in a situation where every day, rockets are fired into Israel while the US tries to pressure the Israelis into a peace process? A Palestinian Authority ambassador said, "There is no difference between Fatah and Hamas. We both agree Israel has no right to exist." Somebody ought to have the courage to tell the truth: These people are terrorists. They teach terrorism in their schools. They have textbooks that say, "If there are 13 Jews and nine Jews are killed, how many Jews are left?" We pay for those textbooks through our aid money. It's time for somebody to have the guts to stand up and say, "Enough lying about the Middle East."

Source: Yahoo's "Your Voice Your Vote" debate in Iowa, Dec. 10, 2011

NOTE: Britain controlled both Israel and Palestine as a colony known as "The British Mandate in Palestine" prior to 1948. On May 14, 1948, the United Nations (with US support, but without Arab support) declared the region partitioned into two states, Israel and Palestine. Neighboring Arab countries immediately invaded; Israel survived the ensuing war but Palestine did not. Gingrich claims that "Palestine" does not exist; he means that it was only an independent legal nation for a very brief period in 1948. But the "Palestinian" identity did exist prior to 1948, and has become the self-identification of Arabs living within the current Israeli borders.

Romney on International Diplomacy

Encourage others to welcome democracy, without military

Q: President Bush said in his second inaugural address, "It is the policy of the US to seek and support the growth of democratic movements and institutions in every nation and culture." Has President Bush's policy been a success, with all the elections going on?

A: Democracy is not defined by a vote. There have to be the underpinnings of democracy: education, health care, people recognizing they live in a place that has the rule of law. And that's why our effort to spread democracy should continue, not to just spread votes, but instead to encourage other people in the world to have the benefits that we enjoy and to welcome democracy. There's no question in this country, we need to reach out, not just with our military might—although that we have, and should keep it strong—but also reach out with our other great capabilities.

Q: Did President Bush fail to appreciate the nuance you're talking about now?

A: I'm not a carbon copy of President Bush. And there are things I would do differently.

Source: GOP Iowa Straw Poll debate, Aug. 5, 2007

Gingrich on International Diplomacy

We need a dramatically expanded use of statecraft

Sen. DODD: Why aren't we using statecraft? What's happened to the utilization of other tools available to us—our economic, our political, our diplomatic resources—which are almost been neglected in this entire process?

GINGRICH: I partially agree with Sen. Dodd. I am not comfortable either with the current situation in Iraq, nor am I comfortable around the world with our extraordinarily limited use of statecraft. The North Koreans are cheating on their agreement on nuclear weapons. We still do not have control of Waziristan in northwest Pakistan, where Bin Laden's probably hiding. We have been told by the UN that the Iranians are now producing at least 1300 centrifuges, producing nuclear material, and that they almost certainly will have a nuclear weapon within a year. You look around the world, the forces of freedom are on retreat, the forces that are anti-freedom, pro-dictatorship, and, in some cases, purely evil are on offense. We need a dramatically expanded ability to use statecraft.

Source: Meet the Press: "Meet the Candidates" series,
May 20, 2007

Romney on the Patriot Act

No Miranda rights for suicide bombers

Before we move away from this "No" epithet that the Democrats are fond of trying to apply to us, let's ask the Obama folks why they say no: no to a balanced budget, no to reforming entitlements, no to malpractice reform, no to missile defense in eastern Europe, no to prosecuting Khalid Sheikh Mohammed in a military tribunal.

Conservatism has had from its inception vigorously positive, intellectually rigorous agenda and thinking. That agenda should have, mind you, three pillars: strength in the economy, strength in our security and strength in our families.

We will strengthen our security by building missile defense, restoring our military might and standing by and strengthening our intelligence officers. Conservatives believe in providing constitutional rights to our citizens, not to enemy combatants like Khalid Sheikh Mohammed.

Not on our watch. A conversation with a would-be suicide bomber will not begin with the words, "You have the right to remain silent."

Source: Speech to Conservative Political Action Conference,
Feb 20, 2010

Gingrich on the Patriot Act

Defend America & allies with information policies

We must implement policies that will ensure America's leadership, safety, and prosperity. To achieve this future we will defend America and our allies from those who would destroy us. To achieve security, we will develop the intelligence, diplomatic, information, defense, and homeland security systems and resources for success.

Source: Gingrich Communications website, www.newt.org, Dec. 1, 2006

All of us will be in danger for the rest of our lives

I think looking at [terrorism] carefully [we should] extend [the PATRIOT Act] and build an honest understanding that all of us will be in danger for the rest of our lives. This is not going to end in the short run. And we need to be prepared to protect ourselves from those who, if they could, would not just kill us individually, but would take out entire cities.

Source: CNN National Security GOP primary debate, Nov. 22, 2011

Romney on Defense Spending

Increase defense spending to at least 4% of GDP

In the face of Obama's approach and foreign policy agenda, we need to do several things. The first is fairly elementary: We should treat our allies like the allies they are. That means, for starters, not being harder on them, or demanding more from them, than we do from our adversaries.

To ensure that America remains safe and maintains its role as a defender of freedom, we also need to increase our defense spending to at least 4% of our GDP per year, including substantial and increasing support for missile defense. Under President Obama, our defense spending will decline as a share of our economy and of the federal budget. And it will fall far below what is required to meet our global commitments.

Source: No Apology, by Mitt Romney, pp. 30-2, March 2, 2010

NOTES: America's GDP (Gross Domestic Product) stands at $14.7 trillion in 2012, according to *CIA World Factbook*. Gov. Romney's suggestion that we spend 4% of GDP on defense spending would mean a defense budget of $588 billion. President Obama's 2013 budget proposal includes $524 billion for defense, or 3.6% of GDP. Hence Romney would spend $64 billion more on defense than Obama in 2013.

Obama further proposes slowing the growth of defense spending in future years. Obama would increase the defense budget by 2% per year, while the CBO projects GDP to grow at about 3% per year. In 2017, Obama proposes $568 billion. Applying Romney's 4% target on 2017 GDP of about $17 trillion would mean $681 billion on defense. Hence Romney would spend $113 billion more on defense than Obama in 2017.

Gingrich on Defense Spending

Defense as percentage of GDP is lowest since WWII

Q: How do you weigh the cost of fighting the war on terror against the exploding debt crisis?

GINGRICH: The exploding debt crisis is because of exploding politician spending in Washington, not because of national security.

Sen. RICK SANTORUM: The first priority of the federal government is to keep America safe. I would not cut defense—freeze it; cut waste; and then plow savings back into Defense.

Gov. GARY JOHNSON: The debt is the greatest threat to national security we face today. Besides, we do not need 60,000 to 100,000 troops in Afghanistan and Iraq to protect ourselves. Nor do we need nation-building.

GINGRICH: We spend less on defense today as percentage of GDP than at any time since Pearl Harbor.

SANTORUM: The first priority of the federal government is to keep America safe. I would not cut defense—freeze it; cut waste; and then plow savings back into Defense.

GINGRICH: Controlling the border and defending America are job #1 under the Constitution.

Source: Republican primary debate on Twitter.com, July 21, 2011

Romney on Sources of Terrorism

To win the war on jihad, we need friends in Muslim world

To win the war on jihad, we have to not only have a strong military of our own—and we need a stronger military—we also need to have strong friends around the world and help moderate Muslims reject the extreme. Because ultimately the only people who can finally defeat these radical Islamic jihadists are the Muslims themselves.

Source: GOP Iowa Straw Poll debate, Aug. 5, 2007

American resolve in Iraq counters jihad with fortitude

The jihadists' history with America justifies their confidence that we will abandon the fight. In 1983, jihadists attacked US marines in Lebanon—and we withdrew. The again in 1993, jihadists attacked US marines in Somalia—and we withdrew. In 2000, jihadists audaciously attacked the USS Cole, killing 17 American sailors, but we did nothing.

With all this history as a backdrop for their lectures to the young, jihadists have become quite confident in the knowledge that, time and again, we have underestimated their threat, their capacity to kill, and their steadfast resolve. This is a lesson they pass on to the young radicals in the making. Only in recent years has American resolve in Iraq and Afghanistan provided a counterexample of Western fortitude in the face of jihadist attacks.

Source: No Apology, by Mitt Romney, p. 71, March 2, 2010

Gingrich on Sources of Terrorism

The "Irreconcilable Wing of Islam" threatens our way of life

Beyond the Petraeus Report, we need a report on the larger war with the Irreconcilable Wing of Islam. This enemy is irreconcilable with the modern civilized world because its values would block any woman from being in this room, having a job, voting, being education. It is irreconcilable because it cannot tolerate other religions or other lifestyles. It represents what some have called an Islamofascist approach to imposing its views on others and as such it is a moral threat to our way of life, to freedom, and to the rule of law.

The Irreconcilable Wing of Islam has emerged as an extremist movement against not only non-Muslims but also against moderate Muslims who wish both to preserve their faith and to be a part of the modern world.

Source: Real Change, by Newt Gingrich, p.292, Dec. 18, 2007

Romney on Afghanistan War

Stay in Afghanistan until our generals say to leave

Q: Osama bin Laden is dead. We've been in Afghanistan for ten years. Isn't it time to bring our combat troops home from Afghanistan?

ROMNEY: It's time for us to bring our troops home as soon as we possibly can, consistent with the word that comes to our generals that we can hand the country over to the Afghan military to defend themselves from the Taliban. I think we've learned some important lessons in our experience in Afghanistan. I want those troops to come home based upon not politics, not based upon economics, but instead based upon the conditions on the ground determined by the generals. But I also think we've learned that our troops shouldn't go off and try and fight a war of independence for another nation. Only the Afghanis can win Afghanistan's independence from the Taliban.

Q: Congressman Paul, do you agree with that decision?

PAUL: Not quite. I make the decisions. I tell the generals what to do. I'd bring them home as quickly as possible.

Source: GOP primary debate in Manchester NH, June 13, 2011

Gingrich on Afghanistan War

We have mismanaged region-wide crisis in Middle East

Q: When should our 90,000 troops in Afghanistan should be brought home?

GINGRICH: I think we're asking the wrong questions. Afghanistan is a tiny piece of a gigantic mess that is very dangerous. Pakistan is unstable and they probably have between 100 and 200 nuclear weapons. Iran is actively trying to get nuclear weapons. They go out and practice closing the Strait of Hormuz, where one out of every six barrels of oil goes through every day. You have the Muslim Brotherhood winning the elections in Egypt. The truth is, we don't know who's in charge in Libya. You have a region-wide crisis, which we have been mismanaging and underestimating, which is not primarily a military problem. We're not going to go in and solve Pakistan militarily. We're not going to go in and solve all these other things. We need a fundamentally new strategy for the region comparable to what we developed to fight the cold war. And I think it's a very big, hard, long-term problem, but it's not primarily a military problem.

Source: WMUR GOP New Hampshire debate, Jan. 7, 2012

Romney on America vs. Socialism

Critical time for American century vs. European socialism

The people of America recognize that this is a critical time. This is not just an average election. This is a time where we're going to decide whether America will remain the great hope of the 21st century, whether this will be an American century, or, instead, whether we'll continue to go down a path to become more and more like Europe, a social welfare state. That's where we're headed. Our economy is becoming weaker. The foundation of our future economy is being eroded. Government has become too large. We're headed in a very dangerous direction.

I believe, to get America back on track, we're going to have to have dramatic, fundamental, extraordinary change in Washington to be able to allow our private sector to once again reemerge competitively, to scale back the size of government and to maintain our strength abroad in our military capacities. I believe that, to change Washington in such a dramatic way, you cannot do it by people who have been there their entire careers.

Source: CNN GOP primary debate on the eve of Florida primary,
Jan 26, 2012

NOTE: "Socialism" is represented by a legal political party in the United States, and in numerous countries abroad. The Socialist Party of America runs candidates for president (Brian Moore in 2008, for example), and has numerous elected mayors around the country. When Pres. Obama is accused of "moving the country toward socialism," his accusers do not imply that he is secretly a member of the Socialist Party, but do imply that he ascribes to that party's beliefs. Those beliefs focus on high progressive taxation; redistribution of wealth; and providing a wide array of social services free of charge.

Gingrich on America vs. Socialism

Is Obama a socialist? "Sure, of course he is"

Q: [to Romney]: When Speaker Gingrich was asked if he believes Pres. Obama is a socialist, he responded, quote, "Sure, of course he is."

ROMNEY: Pres. Obama takes his political inspiration from the socialist democrats in Europe. Guess what? Europe isn't working in Europe. It's not going to work here.

Source: GOP Google debate in Orlando FL, Sept. 22, 2011

Many newspaper editorial boards contain socialists

The Speaker roiled the waters when he told a group of business leaders that many newspaper editorial boards contain socialists. But isn't it possible—even likely—that the Washington Post's editorial board includes a person who endorses a guaranteed annual income, or share-the-wealth schemes, or nationalizing some industries?

To call someone socialist is not necessarily to questions that person's patriotism. In the press reaction to the socialist tag was the suggestion that somehow Gingrich was reviving McCarthyism. It is a case of the offended protesting too much. Socialism has a lengthy American tradition, even if it is now on the wane. After all, President Clinton's Secretary of Labor, Robert Reich, proudly called himself a democratic socialist in the days after his Rhodes scholarship. As Gingrich said, "I'd be glad to get you a collection of editorials that only make senses if people believe that government's good and the free market is bad."

Source: Newt!, by Dick Williams, pp.158-9, June 1, 1995

Book Reviews

OnTheIssues excerpts political books and debates as the primary source of the materials in this book. Following are several book reviews, plus links online to additional political biographies cited in this book.

Book reviews:

Additional book excerpts online:

Book Review:
A Nation Like No Other:
Why American Exceptionalism Matters
by Speaker Newt Gingrich
(June 13, 2011)

The concept of "American Exceptionalism" will permeate the 2011-2012 GOP primary, and likely the 2012 general election as well. Newt Gingrich attempts to out-exception his GOP rivals here, by dedicating an entire book to the concept. We surveyed our non-pundit readers and discovered that the term itself has not yet entered the general voter lexicon—so we will first define it and then analyze its implications here, in anticipation of its usage in upcoming debates.

American exceptionalism means that America has a unique status in the world today, as the sole superpower, and that U.S. policy should work towards recognizing and maintaining that unique status. In contrast to previous nations which ruled the world, America is non-imperialist: previous nations ruled "empires" by occupying territory for the gain of the occupying nation, whereas America establishes bases abroad to enforce the rule of international law and to secure democracy.

Gingrich's definition focuses on the necessary military buildup required to maintain America's unique role (p. 164), as well as on a spiritual basis as its underlying cause (p. 21 & 85). Gingrich previously authored a book, Real Change, expounding upon the need for a larger military; and wrote another book, Rediscovering God in America, outlining the spiritual basis of American society; this book joins those two themes together.

The GOP's interest in American exceptionalism counters Obama's rejection of the concept. When asked in 2009, Obama responded, "Sure, I believe in American exceptionalism in the same way the British believe in British exceptionalism and the Greeks believe in Greek exceptionalism." Republicans generally interpret that as meaning, "No, I don't believe in your version of American exceptionalism at all."

The GOP infers in that disagreement a self-fulfilling prophecy that America is in decline; i.e., that by denying America's role as the sole international superpower, America will eventually doom herself to not being the sole international superpower.

The Left—and Ron Paul—view American exceptionalism as just another form of imperialism. Does it matter to the people of Saudi Arabia that our bases there "protect" them from enemies in common with their dictator's enemies? Do the people of Cuba feel like the U.S. military base at Guantanamo Bay is not a land grab like any other historical invasion? No, say Chomsky and others, all imperialists justified their invasions as for the good of the world, and probably meant it as much as America does today.

Gingrich chose to publish this book at the start of the primary campaign, hence positioning American Exceptionalism as the theme for his presidential candidacy. Ron Paul warns the opposite of Gingrich's recommendation of American Exceptionalism: If America unilaterally maintains a large military abroad, America will collapse economically.

We'll see in a few decades whether Gingrich or Ron Paul were right. But I suspect we'll see in a few months that Gingrich was wrong about making Exceptionalism his campaign theme. Gingrich brilliantly implemented the Contract With America in 1984, with his hand solidly on the pulse of the electorate. But now, not only is Gingrich's hand no longer on the electorate's pulse, but Gingrich seems to not even know where to find their wrist at all. This book just screams "out of touch with the American public."

Book review written July 2011;
full excerpts available online at:
www.ontheissues.org/Nation_No_Other.htm

Book Review:
Turnaround:
Crisis, Leadership, and the Olympic Games
by Gov. Mitt Romney
(June 15, 2004)

This book is about Mitt Romney's experience as the chairman of the Salt Lake Organizing Committee (SLOC), which ran the Salt Lake City Winter Olympic Games in 2002. Some of Romney's comments in the book hail back to his time at Bain Capital, or forward to his time as Governor of Massachusetts. But mostly it's about SLOC, so most of our excerpts are about the principles & values he developed and/or describes from there.

Romney is widely credited with "turning around" the Olympics, after a series of scandals within SLOC involving corruption and bad financial planning. Romney overcame both problems, and pulled off a successful Olympics, which was viewed as having recovered the integrity of the Games, while also turning a profit.

Romney's performance in the Olympics was exemplary and outstandingly positive. However, he claims he never thought about the political implications of running the Olympics; and he claims he never considered running for Governor while at the Olympics. I don't believe that for one second. Romney ran for Senate against Ted Kennedy in the 1990s, and made a decent showing against the single most entrenched incumbent in the Senate. Everyone in Massachusetts politics, including myself, always assumed Romney would run for office again, and fully expected him to segue from the Olympics to a gubernatorial run. If Romney was surprised by that turn of events, he was the only one!

Romney, in effect, rode the coattails of his Olympic turnaround to victory in the Massachusetts gubernatorial election of 2002. There was no gap between the two—Romney flew back from Utah and immediately entered the gubernatorial race. Similarly, there was no gap after Romney retired from the Governor's position—he announced for President the day after the inauguration of Deval Patrick, his successor. So Romney is still, in effect, riding the coattails of the Olympics in the presidential race.

P.S. Full disclosure: I worked as a senior (paid) staffer for the Robert Reich for Governor campaign, which was a Democratic campaign in the primary when Romney was the only Republican candidate. After Reich's loss in the primary, I volunteered with the Shannon O'Brien campaign, which directly ran against Romney in the general election.

Book review written May 2011;
full excerpts available online at:
www.ontheissues.org/No_Apology.htm

Book Review:
No Apology:
The Case for American Greatness
by Gov. Mitt Romney
(March 2, 2010)

This book, published in 2010, outlines Mitt Romney's case against Obama for the 2012 election. Its title makes Romney's case that Obama is an apologist for America (pp.24-33) whereas Romney would instead "proudly defend her." If the title sounds arrogant, that too is Romney's intent: he claims that Obama is too weak in missile defense (p. 18); in defense spending (p. 31); in the War on Terror (p. 64); and in just about everything.

While this book focuses heavily on foreign policy and military issues, Romney also makes the domestic case against Obama. Romney reinforces his conservative credentials against abortion (p. 265) and against gay marriage (p. 269), since those credentials need substantial reinforcement in the view of many hard-line conservatives (Romney ran against Ted Kennedy for the Massachusetts Senate seat in 1994 as a pro-gay, pro-choice Republican).

But mostly Romney focuses on healthcare. And mostly he focuses on how RomneyCare (the Massachusetts healthcare plan initiated by Romney as Governor) is not the same as ObamaCare (p. 176). Mostly Romney's opponents will focus on how ObamaCare is based heavily on RomneyCare: the 2012 Republican primary voters will have to decide which view prevails.

On the question of whether Romney is running in 2012, this book answers unambiguously "Yes." Romney never actually *says* that, of course. But candidates never do. The book's purpose is to establish Romney as sharing core conservative values, which he will need to win the primary election. And the book's other purpose is to establish Romney's line of attack against Obama, which he will need to win the general election. In summary, this book outlines Romney's campaign plans for 2012.

Book review written May 2011;
full excerpts available online at:
www.ontheissues.org/No_Apology.htm

Book Review:
Real Change:
From the World that Fails
to the World that Works
by Speaker Newt Gingrich
(Dec. 18, 2007)

The Republican Party has failed in implementing the Revolution of 1994, and it's time to restart that Revolution again (p. 71). At least, according to Newt Gingrich, who considers himself the architect of the Revolution of 1994. This book was written in 2009, so it's unclear whether Newt considers the Tea Party to be the new Revolution (his partner in the Revolution of 1994, Rep. Dick Armey, certainly does, as outlined in his 2010 book, Give Us Liberty). It is *not* unclear, however, that Newt considers himself to be the appropriate leader for the new Revolution.

The new Revolution is needed now, says Newt, because of the losses to Obama and the Democrats: "For a number of years I kept quiet, but the recent devastation to my party is now so great that I am compelled to speak out explicitly and decisively." (p. 24). He blames partisanship on both sides of the aisle (p. 43) for the dysfunctional state of American politics: he has one chapter entitled "An Unreformed Right: Why Republicans Can't Govern Successfully"; and another entitled "An Unreformed Left: Why Democrats Can't Deliver Real Change." The solution? Go back to the non-partisanship of the Revolution of 1994.

Citizens who actually remember the Revolution of 1994, in contrast to Newt, generally consider the era to be quite partisan. Newt *does* deserve credit for "nationalizing" the Congressional election of 1994 (getting people to vote for the Contract With America as much as just for their individual Congressional race); and he *does* deserve credit for a Revolution. But he also deserves blame for the harsh partisanship that characterized the House of Representatives in the

1990s, culminating in Bill Clinton's impeachment, arguably the most partisan act in American history. Citizens might also contrast Newt's view with the fact that he resigned from the House speakership in the wake of a government shutdown—also an intensely partisan act.

Nevertheless, Newt is back, and he is running for President. This book is just the first salvo in his battle for the GOP nomination. He has prepared appropriately: he formed several political organizations in the past decade to bolster his credentials on key issues (each of which gets a plug for its website, p. xxi):

- The Center for Health Transformation (www. HealthTransformation.net)

- American Solutions for Winning the Future (www. AmericanSolutions.com)

- Renewing American Leadership (ReAL, www.RenewingAmericanLeadership.com)

If Newt does enter the Republican primary, he is sure to be great entertainment. While Newt is renowned for his slightly non-mainstream academic analysis, listeners accept it as mainstream because he delivers it with such certitude (almost always in this book, the passive voice is used, to illustrate how it's obvious that most voters are in agreement). His analysis is data-driven and historical (he's a history professor, after all), although some might call that "wonkish," a sure-fire losing attitude since Dukakis' days. Newt would call his attitude "futuristic," since his hero is still Alvin Toffler, author of *Future Shock* and *The Third Wave* (p. 65).

Whether wonkish or futuristic, Newt will be non-mainstream and hence entertaining. For example, he proposes (in the passive voice) that the US should invade Pakistan: "Afghanistan would have been dealt with in a regional context that would have included the Waziristan section of Pakistan." (p. 305). And maybe invade Syria and others too (also in the passive voice): "There would have been no free passage through Damascus for foreign terrorists to come kill Americans," but that wouldn't actually require invasions because the dictators might yield once they saw "the fury of the American people mobilized to action."

In summary, Newt positions himself as the conservative choice: more hawkish than the GOP hawks; more anti-Obama than the rest of the GOP; and more "change" than Obama ever offered. Newt will have a lot of trouble with the conservatives accepting his three divorces; he'll have even more trouble with the general electorate accepting his conversion to non-partisanship; and he'll have the most trouble of all with voters who remember him as the past generation instead of the future. But he'll be a heck of a lot of fun!

Book review written April 2011;
full excerpts available online at:
www.ontheissues.org/Real_Change.htm

Book Review:
Rediscovering God in America:
Reflections on the Role of Faith in
Our Nation's History and Future
by Speaker Newt Gingrich
(Oct. 10, 2006)

Newt Gingrich in this book expresses strongly how important God has been to American history. The structure of this book is a "tour" of Washington DC, pointing out all of the references to God built into our public monuments and buildings, as well as in their design and history. The details of that aspect of the book are mostly omitted here because OnTheIssues doesn't have categories for history nor architecture.

But there is a political purpose too, and those comprise our excerpts. In particular, Gingrich applies the historical importance of God in America to examine numerous current public policy issues, from the Pledge of Allegiance to school prayer. Gingrich reserves particular venom for the US Supreme Court and other courts who rule in favor of omitting God from public displays—claiming that they are usurping power intended for the legislature, and also ignoring the importance of God in centuries of American history.

This book is similar in conclusions to Mike Huckabee's *Character Makes a Difference*. Gov. Huckabee, however, comes from a pastoral perspective, arguing on religious and moral grounds instead of Gingrich's historical grounds. Gingrich's argument is certainly more effective when attempting to persuade non-Christians or secularists.

Book review written May 2007;
full excerpts available online at:
www.ontheissues.org/Rediscovering_God.htm

Book Review:
Newt!
Leader of the Second
American Revolution
by Dick Williams
(June 1995)

This book was written in 1995, when Newt Gingrich's was the newly-elected Speaker of the House. He had just engineered the Republican takeover of the House of Representatives, and had not yet fallen from power after struggles with President Bill Clinton. Hence this book is a snapshot of Newt at the peak of his power. If Newt runs for President in 2012, as currently seems likely, this book will become a valuable indicator of his views before any post-Clinton lessons.

The book is important for two reasons in the 2012 presidential race: it pinpoints where Newt stands on the scale of conservatism; and demonstrates the consistency of his political views over time. A few words on each...

The 2012 Republican presidential primary will focus on "pure" conservatism vs. pragmatic electability. The pure conservatives will be the champions of the Tea Party, which currently prefers Governor Sarah Palin but also have a less-controversial option in Governor Mike Huckabee. Their mantra might be "Had enough of Obama? We're the real alternative." The pragmatic electable group is currently led by Governor Mitt Romney, who will be followed by the usual panoply of ambitious Republican Senators and Governors. Their mantra might be "Had enough of Obama? We can actually beat him."

That conflict—ideological purity vs. electability—is the classic conflict for the party challenging an incumbent president. For example, Senator John Kerry (as the pragmatic choice) beat Governor Howard Dean (as the ideological choice) for the 2004 Democratic nomination against Pres. Bush's re-election. Many pundits say that Kerry lost to Bush because Kerry was too pragmatic—or as Bush characterized him, as a waffler on issues who had no core principles. Gov. Dean had flaws, but waffling was not one of them.

The trick to a successful challenge to an incumbent president is to gather support from both groups: the ideologues of your party *and* the pragmatists. Newt Gingrich has positioned himself to fill that niche. He is proudly a partisan conservative, as demonstrated in every excerpt from this book, but is also famously pragmatic—he actually implemented the welfare reform proposed in this book by working with Pres. Clinton. And he accomplished a Republican takeover of the House by proposing a conservative platform, the Contract With America—and then implemented its promises (they only promised to *introduce* legislation; not to actually *pass* it).

The only other candidate who could fill that double-niche is Senator Jim DeMint of South Carolina. Senator DeMint spent most of 2010 campaigning for Tea Party Senate candidates (and DeMint has a book too, *Saving Freedom*). That makes for some powerful allies, and DeMint can point to his election and re-election to the Senate as evidence of pragmatism. But Gingrich is much better-known nationally than DeMint, so it should be an interesting primary.

On Gingrich's consistency of political views: Newt has been criticized often for compromising on core issues, and for changing his views with the political winds. This book addresses that criticism in several contexts, for example by quoting how Gingrich's college lectures match the Contract with America. Newt is safe from this attack, if one looks at the record. He is safe from attack on grounds of over-ideological-purity because he admits in this book to smoking marijuana (p. 19) and to marital infidelity (p. 94). Since he still adheres to the tenets of the Contract With America 15 years later, consistency now seems obvious. Hence Newt is a strong candidate for the double-niche position.

We have added Newt Gingrich to our early Presidential 2012 VoteMatch quiz, where you answer 20 questions and get matched issue-by-issue with the major candidates. All of the candidates for the Republican nomination discussed above are also included in the VoteMatch quiz.

Book review written Nov. 2010;
full excerpts available online at:
www.ontheissues.org/Newt_Revolution.htm

Romney vs. Gingrich on VoteMatch

VoteMatch is our 20-question quiz which summarizes the candidate's views on the controversial issues of the day.

VoteMatch Social Issues

	Mitt Romney	Newt Gingrich
Abortion is a woman's right	opposes	strongly opposes
Require companies to hire more women & minorities	strongly favors	strongly opposes
Same-sex domestic partnership benefits	opposes	opposes
Teacher-led prayer in public schools	strongly favors	strongly favors
Parents choose schools via vouchers	strongly favors	strongly favors

VoteMatch Domestic Issues

	Mitt Romney	Newt Gingrich
More federal funding for health coverage	neutral	strongly opposes
Death Penalty	strongly favors	strongly favors
Mandatory Three Strikes sentencing laws	strongly favors	favors
Absolute right to gun ownership	opposes	favors
Drug use is immoral: enforce laws against it	strongly favors	strongly favors

VoteMatch Economic Issues

	Mitt Romney	Newt Gingrich
Privatize Social Security	strongly favors	strongly favors
Make taxes more progressive	strongly opposes	opposes
Stricter limits on political campaign funds	opposes	strongly opposes
Allow churches to provide welfare services	favors	favors
Replace coal & oil with alternatives	opposes	strongly opposes

VoteMatch International Issues

	Mitt Romney	Newt Gingrich
Illegal immigrants earn citizenship	opposes	neutral
Support & expand free trade	neutral	favors
The Patriot Act harms civil liberties	strongly opposes	strongly opposes
Expand the armed forces	strongly favors	strongly favors
US out of Iraq and Afghanistan	strongly opposes	favors

In our online quiz, you fill in your answers for these 20 questions, and we match you against all the candidates. Please see:

http://quiz.ontheissues.org/

Afterword

We hope that this book encourages you, as voters, to make your decisions based on the issues. We recognize the reality of American politics: voters make their decisions based primarily on whether they like the candidates. Accordingly, our goal is to get voters to compare their issue preferences in comparison to candidate issue stances when considering which candidates to like.

We intentionally omitted from this book any biographical background on Gov. Romney and Speaker Gingrich. Details of their religious affiliations and past marriages—and minutiae of every other personal detail—are readily available in the mainstream media. Their issue stances are more challenging for voters to find.

Why does the mainstream media fail at this important function? Because they are "news" organizations which are poorly suited to covering political campaigns. "News" implies reporting on what is "new": Gingrich's stance on capital punishment has not changed since 1994, and Romney's stance on school vouchers has similarly not changed since 1994, so there's nothing in the news about those issues. But if you are impassioned about the death penalty, or if you vote based on education policy, then you can't rely on the news media for those non-newsworthy issues. And that's where we come in.

This book represents an archive of where these two candidates stand on the key issues of our time. We don't consider whether candidates' issue stances are new—just what they say on each issue. That often requires a lot of digging on our part—we have a team of researchers to do that, but we invite you to volunteer any issue stances that we don't cover.

Our online website www.ontheissues.org covers many more issues than can fit in any book: many more stances from Newt Gingrich and Mitt Romney, as well as all of the other 2012 candidates, Governors, Senators, and House members. We score each candidate on a 20-question quiz called "VoteMatch." A representation of the VoteMatch quiz results for the presidential contenders appears on the back cover of this book. The mainstream media interpret candidates using a one-dimensional "right-left" analysis. That simplistic analysis comes to nonsensical conclusions like calling Ron Paul "extreme right-wing" even though he opposes the Iraq War; opposes the Patriot Act; supports drug legalization; and supports same-sex domestic partnership benefits.

We find our two-dimensional analysis to be more accurate in differentiating candidates than that traditional one-dimensional analysis. We don't claim that our method is perfect—just superior to the simplistic mainstream media. VoteMatch uses a Social Issues dimension plus an Economic Issues dimension; we interpret candidates based on whether they believe in government involvement in either or both of those dimensions. Using the two-dimensional analysis differentiates five classes of political beliefs:

1. *Libertarian:*
   No government involvement in social issues
   No government involvement in economic issues

2. *Conservative:*
   Government involvement in social issues
   No government involvement in economic issues

3. *Liberal:*
   No government involvement in social issues
   Government involvement in economic issues

4. *Populist:*
   Government involvement in social issues
   Government involvement in economic issues

5. *Centrist:*
   Some government involvement in social issues
   Some government involvement in economic issues

Most importantly, you can answer the same 20 questions and see *your* political label and how the candidates match up with *you*. We invite you to try the VoteMatch quiz at:

http://quiz.ontheissues.org

Other Books in This Series

- Rick Perry vs. Mitt Romney On The Issues

- Sarah Palin vs. Michele Bachmann On The Issues

- Mitt Romney vs. Newt Gingrich On The Issues

- Rick Santorum vs. Mitt Romney On The Issues

- Ron Paul vs. Newt Gingrich on The Issues

- Barack Obama vs. Mitt Romney On The Issues

About the Author

Jesse Gordon has been the editor-in-chief of OnTheIssues.org since its formation in 1999. His passion revolves around providing issue-based coverage on political races, to combat the mainstream media's growing lack of such coverage.

Mr. Gordon holds a Master's degree in Public Policy from Harvard University's Kennedy School of Government. He and the website OnTheIssues.org are based in Cambridge, Massachusetts. He resides with his fiancée, Kathleen; his son Julien; Kathleen's son Derek; their cat Chanel; and six fish with whom Chanel is obsessed.

Mr. Gordon replies to email personally, at jesse@ontheissues. org—whether to suggest improvements to the website or to order one of the other books above.